D1416326

3 1520 00029222 7

THE ROLE OF THE
CONGRESSMAN

ROGER H. DAVIDSON

PEGASUS   NEW YORK

THE ROLE OF THE CONGRESSMAN is part of a series, "Studies in Contemporary American Politics," published by Pegasus under the General Editorship of Richard E. Morgan, Columbia University.

TO MY MOTHER AND FATHER

PREFACE

M ost intellectual enterprises are the result of collaboration of one sort or another, and the present book is no exception. This report is part of an extensive research undertaking which has proceeded, albeit discontinuously, over a period of several years. My co-workers in the enterprise have been David M. Kovenock, now director of the Comparative State Elections Project at the University of North Carolina; and Michael K. O'Leary, a professor at the Maxwell Graduate School of Citizenship and Public Service at Syracuse University.

Our collaboration began in February 1963, when we were asked by Professor Gene M. Lyons, director of the Dartmouth Public Affairs Center, to undertake a study of Congressional reform. At the time all of us were members of the faculty at Dartmouth College. Professor Lyons was planning a conference to be held the following year as the first in a series honoring Orvil E. Dryfoos, the late publisher of *The New York Times*. Congressional reform, which had always interested Mr. Dryfoos, seemed a timely and appropriate focus.

As we were well aware, the topic was hardly new. Even the "modern" literature on the subject extended well back into the nineteenth century. Moreover, the writing all too frequently reflected the problems and pitfalls of the political science discipline; and we were unwilling to produce yet another recitation of legislative foibles, yet another academic lecture on the need for reform. Thus we chose to fulfill our assignment by examining the politics of reform—a task we felt might help political scientists and policy-makers alike to understand the dynamics of change in an institution like Congress. Our research has been presented under joint authorship in several separate reports.[1]

A key feature of the research was a sample survey of 116 members of the U.S. House of Representatives, completed in 1963–1964. (The methodology of this survey is explained in detail in the Appendix.) Drawing upon these interviews with Congressmen, we were able to measure the "reform market" that existed in the 88th Congress and map some basic contours of the politics of reform.

Equally significant, however, was the long-range use of our survey instrument to probe the legislators' conceptions of their roles—the ways in which Congressmen view their tasks, the function of the national legislature, and the legitimate place of constituent claims, political parties, and interest groups. Many of our inquiries were suggested by the pioneering work of John Wahlke, Heinz Eulau, William Buchanan, and Leroy C. Ferguson in applying the role-theoretical approach to the study of four state legislatures.[2]

Only a few of the most obvious findings from this phase of the research have been presented in earlier reports. Like the legislators we interviewed, we were beset by other pressing commitments and that universal malady, lack of time. Nevertheless, the desirability of reporting this aspect of the over-all research was recognized. For a variety of reasons, therefore, it seemed the most expedient course for the present author to summarize, somewhat more briefly than originally intended, the findings pertaining to the role prescriptions of Congressmen. Other phases of the research—including investigation of the views of Congress held by the general public, local elites, and the Washington press corps (data for the last having already been gathered)—will have to await further allocations of time and resources.

This book opens with a brief discussion of the concept of the legislator (Chapter 1). From a conceptual point of view the discussion is designed to throw light on what it means to be a legislator, and what behaviors typically accompany this distinctive form of political activity. Legislators will be described as participants in a process of bargaining over society's goal or resource allocations. As bargainers they serve as fiduciary agents for individuals and groups that, though located outside the legislative arena, nonetheless possess real and legitimate claims to be realized through goal allocations. As bargainers legislators tend to develop a distinctive self-image, as well as a set of behavioral norms that they apply to all who hold legislative office. Such role orientations may be well- or ill-suited for satisfactory performance of the legislative function—a problem to be taken up later in the book.

In Chapter 2 we consider several attributes that help to define the status of members of Congress in our social and political system. Selected background characteristics of Representatives and Senators are examined, as are aspects of Congressional career patterns. Data presented in this chapter are drawn from supplementary questionnaires submitted to our respondents in the 88th Congress, as well as from an exploratory historical examination of the membership of ten selected Congresses conducted by the author and his research assistant, Richard C. Neuhoff, in the summer of 1967. Other investigators have discovered that so-called "social background variables" offer scant explanation of legislative role-taking; and the present study, in the main, substantiates their findings. However, such factors—occupational training, political experience, and career patterns, for example—help to illuminate the ways in which legislators respond to their environment in selecting and acting out their roles. Moreover, such factors suggest hypotheses concerning the relative content, strength, and salience of legislators' role prescriptions at different times.

The most inclusive type of role cognition, the purposive role, is examined in Chapter 3. The purposive role represents the Congressman's most generalized response to the question, "What should I do as a legislator?" Another form of job definition— the activities that the member considers to be most important and time-consuming—is also considered.

The legislator-as-representative is the subject of Chapter 4. Two dimensions of the representative function are given particular attention. One is: Does the legislator believe he should act on constituency instructions, or does he see his job as one of making decisions on the basis of his own understanding, insight, or conscience? The divergent styles of representation posed by this question have interested political theorists and practitioners since the rise of modern representative institutions. Equally important is the issue of to *what* constituency the legislator's ear is attuned.

Depending upon his orientations and the exigencies of a specific situation, the legislator's effective constituency may be an electoral district, the nation at large, a specialized policy clientele, or some combination of these. This dimension, which we call the *focus* of representation, is also examined in Chapter 4.

The responses of Congressmen to political party and pressure groups are the concerns of Chapter 5. Here we shall examine the various ways by which legislators relate themselves to these two important aspects of their environment. These role dimensions, far from exhausting the possibilities, are merely representative of a multitude of roles that Congressmen assume in performing the many tasks associated with their formal position in our political system.

Finally, we will attempt in the conclusion to show how these roles are related to one another, as well as to the legislature's function in the political system. Throughout our discussion we will seek to define with as much precision as possible the options available to the legislator, report findings that indicate the proportions of Congressmen choosing each option, and explain (insofar as feasible with a sample of limited size) the forces that induce the legislator to select one option over another. The result of our inquiry, it is hoped, is a fairly consistent picture of the contemporary legislature as a system of role orientations. Whether this role system is well-adapted to the functions of the contemporary Congress—an issue of enormous import for the present and future health of the institution—is a final problem on which we will attempt some informed speculation.

Many persons assisted at various stages of the research and writing to make this book possible. My two colleagues, Professors Kovenock and O'Leary, served with me as co-directors of the research project from which the present data are drawn. Our association has been a long and happy one; and though other commitments prevented their collaboration in the actual writing of this study, these two colleagues have encouraged me to persevere with the research and have offered numerous useful suggestions. Lest they be victims of guilt by association, however, I wish to state that I alone am responsible for the specific interpretations and conclusions offered here.

My colleagues would, I know, want me to reiterate my gratitude to those individuals and institutions whose assistance we acknowledged in our earlier book—particularly to Professor Gene M. Lyons and the Public Affairs Center of Dartmouth College. In addition I wish to offer thanks to my research assistants, Richard C. Neuhoff and Edmund S. Cohen, who demonstrated unflagging zeal and cheerfulness during analysis of the data. Preparation of the manuscript was made possible by a grant from the Faculty Research Committee of Dartmouth College. Several colleagues at other institutions were kind enough to review the manuscript, either in whole or in part, and provide many helpful criticisms and suggestions. These persons included Professors Alan Rosenthal of Rutgers University; John F. Bibby of the University of Wisconsin, Milwaukee; Judson L. James of the City University of New York; Dorothy B. James of Lehman College, City University of New York; and Richard E. Morgan of Columbia University.

My wife Nancy helped immeasurably by making tolerable the sacrifices normally associated with such an enterprise and by offering insights from her own experience on Capitol Hill. My dedication of this book to my parents is but a small expression of my gratitude for the atmosphere of learning that they encourage in their home.

Santa Barbara, California
November 1968

CONTENTS

THE ROLE OF THE
CONGRESSMAN

CHAPTER 1

THE LEGISLATIVE FUNCTION

This is a book about legislators. Specifically, it focuses upon a small but very significant group of legislators—the members of the United States House of Representatives.

Those acquainted with recent studies of Congress but unfamiliar with the vagaries of scholarship may well wonder why, in an era described variously as bureaucratic or antiparliamentary, legislators warrant such relentless scrutiny. Are not students of legislative behavior open to the charge often levelled at the Department of Agriculture: that it grows at a rate equal only to its clientele's rate of decline?

The current vogue of legislative behavior studies is the product of many factors, not the least of which is the unique susceptibility of legislatures to the probing of analytical and empirical tools now used by researchers. Thus, such diverse techniques as voting analysis, small-groups research, and survey research have helped to cast light into the dark corners of the legislative labyrinth. By the same token, conceptual schemes drawn from such varied sources as organization theory, systems theory, and bargaining and games theories have found fertile application. Studies of these types have been encouraged by the fact that legislators' actions and deliberations are relatively open and accessible to the outside observer. Legislators are, by necessity and inclination, "public men"; and the reticence required of bureaucrats and judges is less often required of them. These compelling reasons have persuaded contemporary students to lavish great attention upon legislators and legislative institutions.[1]

Of course such considerations, however persuasive for professional observers, do not in themselves justify interest or concern on the part of informed citizens. The public's knowledge and awareness of legislators, for example, are notoriously low. As young people, citizens tend to learn about high elected executives, such as Presidents and Governors, before they learn about legislators; and children often think of national legislators as "the President's helpers." Not surprisingly, legislators often fare badly at the hands of the popular culture. Mass media frequently neglect legislators: The President, for example, makes better copy. And references to legislators, when they occur, are often tinged with sarcasm that is only partly deserved. Thus the public perceives Congress, if at all, with blurred vision.[2]

Yet the strategic position of the legislator, so ingrained in our historical tradition, forms a key assumption of this and other studies of the subject. To understand who legislators are and how they approach their tasks is to take a large step toward understanding the nature of political life. To explain why this is so, it is useful at the outset to sketch a conceptual picture of the political system and the functions legislators perform in it.

By starting from a broad conceptual framework, the student can expand his vision of political phenomena. The present study, for example, offers only a limited perspective drawn from a narrow range of findings. Specifically, the findings relate to certain characteristics and attitudes of members of the United States House of Representatives. From a conceptual vantage point, however, many of the attributes of Congressmen could just as well apply to legislators in, say, Kansas or India or the Marshall Islands. It was Aristotle who first demonstrated that though political institutions and practices differ greatly among cultures, they can nonetheless be described and categorized by means of universally applied criteria. Thus, while the present subjects comprise a very specific group of men—bounded in time and culture—their attitudes and behaviors may suggest something of what it means to be "a legislator."

THE MEANING OF POLITICS

The primary function of the political system, or polity, is to provide mechanisms for specifying and implementing the goals of the larger society. Indeed, nearly all social theorists associate the important task of goal attainment with the institutions of the polity—which include not only the formal organs of government but also political parties, interest groups, and elite groupings.[3] This conception of politics is not very different from David Easton's now common definition: politics as the authoritative allocation of societal values and resources.[4]

The political function, as William C. Mitchell has pointed out, really embraces a dual problem.[5] First, within a large society of many components operating in an unstable environment, a multiplicity of goals is extremely likely. Thus, the polity must provide mechanisms for setting priorities among the alternative goals. Obviously, some goals will be rejected out of hand. Others may receive only lip service. Still others will be granted varying degrees of support. No matter how efficient, a polity cannot select, nor even process, all the possible goals being urged upon it. Nor will the contributions of society's other components, in the form of resources or support, be sufficient to support maximum or even adequate attention to all possible goals. Some polities are fortunate in possessing great resources for meeting demands; others must operate on more slender resources. But no polity, however impressive its resources, can resolve more than a small portion of the conflicting demands made upon it to pursue various goals.[6]

As a second and related task, the polity must find means of mobilizing the resources or facilities needed to realize the goals that are selected. Administration and co-ordination are required to implement any collective enterprise. And what is more, the numerous goal-oriented segments of the society must be reconciled to the choices that have been made, so that they will consent to whatever sacrifices are required to realize the goals. In reconciling various interests, political structures must possess the quality of legitimacy; that is, they must appear to operate in conformity with the values of the society. In this manner, potentially divisive decisions will assume the character of propriety or justice.

In sum, as Mitchell has stated, choice and economy are inevitable problems that the polity is called upon to confront:

> Because of the multiplicity of goals and the scarcity of means, conflict in some form is an inevitable consequence which the society has to minimize, if it is to survive. If all values or goals cannot be maximized, some means must be developed for their allocation which will be accepted as authoritative.[7]

Conflict is thus a ubiquitous feature of the polity. Its resources and mechanisms for resolving conflict over societal goals are crucial to the long-term stability of the society itself. Moreover, proponents of various goal priorities tend to evaluate political structures at least partially in terms of their success in meeting special demands.[8] Indeed, many seemingly minor issues are actually conflicts over the priorities to be assigned to public goals, or over the distribution of costs and responsibilities for their attainment.

The polity's outputs are in the currency of power, in the concrete form of *decisions* or *policies*—which, taken as a whole, define the goal priorities of the society. These priorities are expressed in directives that demand action, or restraint from action, on the part of citizens. Such directives appear in a variety of forms: as laws or regulations, judicial decisions, or executive orders of various kinds. In a large and complex society they are usually drafted in great detail and rationalized by their consistency with norms of the polity and the society as a whole.

The internal structure of the political system is quite varied, in part because it faces a variety of functional problems.[9] If a polity is to survive, it must cope with the problems of adaptation to its environment (including the environment internal to the society), goal attainment, integration of conflict, and maintenance of traditional patterns of behavior. These problems tend to shape the structure of the polity; and in advanced polities specialized structures emerge to deal with them. In turn, these structures contain specialized subgroupings. To refer to the example at hand, the legislature is but one aspect (albeit an unusually visible one) of the polity; but the legislature itself is divided into specialized subunits of such complexity that even members of Congress require years to understand their workings.

The Parsons-Mitchell paradigm of polity functions, with slight modifications, is characterized in Table 1-1. Even the casual student of the American scene will recognize here a familiar division of functions. Familiarity can be deceptive, however, for these structures reflect only partly the "bricks-and-mortar" institutions of the high school civics curriculum—that is, executive, legislative, and judicial. Congress is primarily a legislative structure, for example, but it often performs administrative, executive, or judicial functions. Nor is this some aberration of Constitutional theory: The Constitution itself gives Congress judicial powers (as in trials of impeachment) and administrative powers (as in the raising and equipping of armies). What is true of Congress is equally true of other institutions. This is why bargaining among agencies within the executive branch is sometimes referred to as "legislation," and why the courts are often (and sometimes rightly) described as legislative bodies.

Table 1–1. Function and Structure in the Polity

System Function	Structure
Adaptation	Administration
Goal Attainment	Executive Leadership
Integration	Legislative, Political parties
Pattern-maintenance	Judicial

The model implies not that a political structure is exclusively devoted to performing a given function, but rather that it is *characteristically* directed at such a function. This refinement enables us to go at least one significant step beyond a simplistic institutional delineation of function. It permits, first of all, a specification of the central, or quintessential, nature of the structure in relation to political functions. It provides, moreover, a conceptual method of analyzing the extent to which these functions are performed by *other* structures within the polity. In this way we may avoid the tyranny of institutional nomenclature, which tells us merely that the legislature makes laws, the executive executes, and so on. This conceptual refinement is again not inconsistent with Constitutional theory. Whatever conventional wisdom may dictate on the matter, the Founding Fathers clearly envisioned a polity, not of separate structures performing separate functions, but of separate structures *sharing* functions. As James Madison expressed it, the Constitution created a government of blended powers.[10]

The legislature, in terms of this model, is primarily an institution that contributes to the attainment of goals by securing support and integrating conflicts among members of the system. To be sure, political structures often compete with each other over the performance of functions. Many of the recurrent debates over the legitimate boundaries of institutional powers are in fact contests over the degree of monopoly that an institution may legitimately exercise over a given function. Such debates are "Constitutional conflicts" in the deepest sense of the term.

THE CONCEPT OF THE LEGISLATOR

What, then, are the distinctive features of legislative behavior? Or the question might be put, What does it mean to be a legislator? What sets legislators apart from other political actors? And conversely, under what conditions do other actors—who are not legislators in any institutional sense—actually engage in legislative behavior? In the remainder of this chapter a tentative conceptual answer to these queries will be ventured; in the chapters to follow, this answer will be probed by an examination of several related sets of empirical data.

Based on the foregoing discussion, we can venture the following statements concerning the nature of the legislative system. First, as a distinctive system of behaviors within the polity, legislating is a type of goal specification which emphasizes the resolving of conflict among various contesting collectivities. Second, the key inputs of legislation are (a) many goal-oriented demands, (b) limited and dispersed resources for meeting those demands, and (c) changing levels of support from citizens and groups. From these ingredients the legislative process must devise, or at least lend support to, authoritative decisions that are accepted by citizens (or a significant proportion of them) and are at least symbolically directed toward goals. As Roland Young has characterized the legislative task:

> Congress is chiefly concerned with resolving conflict by establishing a pattern of legal order which those affected are constrained to follow, and it resolves such conflict by establishing generalized rules ordinarily administered by the governmental bureaucracy. In order to operate as a legislature capable of resolving conflict, Congress must develop an internal system of authority and action as well as establish communications with the external world.[11]

The system achieves a degree of closure because outputs exert a "feedback" effect upon future inputs. That is, the kinds of decisions a legislature makes will have a decided impact upon subsequent demands, resources, and support levels. A simple diagram will help to illustrate these relationships (Figure 1-A).

Figure 1-A. The Legislative System

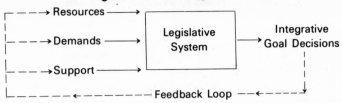

For the purpose of describing legislative behavior, the most important features of a legislator's environment are, first, that imperfect agreement exists upon the goals to be realized and, second, that resources for influencing these goals are widely distributed among the actors. These two conditions, in fact, are prerequisites for a system of legislative behaviors. By the same token, the behaviors that emerge as distinctively "legislative" in character are responses to these facts of political life. These behaviors are broadly subsumed under the concept of "bargaining." Congress is thus "an influence system in which bargain and exchange predominate." [12]

Two necessary qualifications must be introduced. First, although these two conditions—disagreement on goals and widely distributed resources—are necessary conditions for legislative behavior, they are rarely if ever met perfectly in complex human situations. This cautionary statement refers merely to the fact that pure behavior types are rarely found in the real world. A second qualification is that although bargaining behaviors predominate in legislative institutions, they are also present to a greater or lesser degree in other settings, both political and nonpolitical.

In order to clarify these qualifications, it is useful to visualize the types of behaviors that occur when the two key variables, goals and resources, are manipulated.* The model is set forth in Table 1-2. As goal and resource inputs are altered, so are the resulting political behaviors. Under this conceptualization, there are four typical political relationships: problem-solving; command; leadership, or persuasion; and bargaining.

The problem-solving situation conforms to the classic model of

*The input of support will here be assumed as constant. Although levels of support do fluctuate, they must remain sufficient to assure continuation of the behavioral relationship. What the model assumes, therefore, is that the relationships are not in danger of dissolving —though in fact this condition may occur in the real world.

Table 1–2. Types of Political Relationships

RESOURCES	GOALS	
	Shared	*Unshared*
Equal	Problem-solving	Bargaining
Unequal	Leadership-Persuasion	Command

rational-comprehensive decision-making. If the actors are relatively equal in the resources they bring to a situation, and if they are agreed upon the goal of their enterprise, their task is in theory quite simple. They merely have to sit down and explore the means to their goal. The stratagem is particularly appropriate when the goal being pursued is instrumental and not a broad end-goal. Picture, for instance, a group of skilled technicians convened to devise a better mousetrap. If their firm makes mousetraps, they need not dispute whether mice are desirable creatures, or even whether some other form of control—e.g., chemicals— might not be more effective. They need only bring their skills to bear on the problem at hand. This happy situation has been envisioned by political philosophers at least since Plato introduced the concept of the Philosopher-Ruler. And it has constituted a portion of the mythology once associated with judicial decisionmaking, in which the judge was viewed merely as comparing the case in dispute with immutable legal principles. Although the problem-solving pattern may be approximated in a number of group situations, it certainly occurs less frequently than the theorists of rationalism would prefer. And even when the conditions are initially present, the situation is quickly contaminated when the participants develop personal attachments to given solutions. (i.e., mediate goals).*

The opposite situation exists when goals are unshared and resources are highly unequal (that is, distributed hierarchically). This results in a command relationship, wherein those who possess resources must coerce the other actors to move in the direc-

---

*Froman makes the point somewhat differently: "The more organizational conflict represents individual rather than intergroup conflict, the greater the use of analytic procedures. The more organizational conflict represents intergroup differences, the greater the use of bargaining." [13]

tion of a given goal. Here, too, the conditions are rarely present in pure form. For example, a military officer must see to it that his orders are carried out, even when his men find them unpleasant or dangerous. Yet no officer can rely on coercion alone. Rather, he will attempt to enhance compliance with orders by resorting to persuasion or bargaining. To ignore such factors as the goals and resources of his men (taken collectively) would be to risk noncompliance.

In political life especially, the command situation is rarely approximated because its preconditions are rarely met. One is reminded of the amusement with which President Truman contemplated how his Army-trained successor, Eisenhower, would approach the Presidency. As Richard E. Neustadt reports the incident, Truman tapped his desk for emphasis and remarked: "He'll sit here and he'll say, 'Do this! Do that!' *And nothing will happen.* Poor Ike—it won't be a bit like the Army. He'll find it very frustrating." [14] This was a recognition that the Presidency, like most political situations, is not primarily a matter of command but of persuasion and bargaining—a theme which Neustadt pursues with great insight.

Although problem-solving and command might appear to be relatively trouble-free mechanisms for allocating goals and mobilizing resources, they are relatively unreliable. Problem-solving quickly degenerates into other relationships because the actors soon display disparities in resources and disagreement over instrumental goals. Command, too, must be employed with extreme caution because the resources of the disadvantaged actors, however small when taken individually, may when pooled be significant. The would-be commander must thus resort to persuasion or bargaining in order to maximize the compliance, not to mention the morale, of the other actors. If naked command is resorted to, it may be a painful last resort, "suggestive less of mastery than failure—the failure of attempts to gain an end by softer means." [15]* All human relationships are therefore likely to include aspects of leadership and bargaining, both of which—as will be seen—involve the *manipulation* of goals and resources. To this extent all relation-

*Although the Presidency, for example, confers such impressive resources that elements of command are perhaps more prevalent than Neustadt's analysis suggests, his assessment is nonetheless valid: "Command is but a method of persuasion, not a substitute, and not a method suitable for everyday employment." [16]

ships contain elements of politics. But nowhere is this more conspicuous than in polity relationships, which by definition involve
disparities in these crucial inputs.

In those situations commonly called "political," leadership or
bargaining relationships predominate. Leadership might be called
the mobilization of resources through an exploration of consensus.
A leadership may include elements of command, bargaining, or
problem-solving, it is primarily an appeal to the shared goals
of the group—often through the manipulation of verbal symbols.
Again it is instructive to turn to the insight of President Truman,
who remarked that "I spend most of my time here telling people
to do what they ought to have sense enough to do anyway." Or,
as Neustadt expresses it, "The essence of a President's persuasive
task with congressmen and everybody else, *is to induce them to
believe that what he wants of them is what their own appraisal of their
own responsibilities requires them to do in their interest, not his.*"[17]*As
we have already observed, a command relationship may shift to
one of leadership as soon as the dominant actor recognizes the
necessity of going beyond coercion to influence the actions of
others.

The final relationship, bargaining, is a political situation *par
excellence.* It is distinguished, as we have said, by imperfectly shared
goals and widely distributed resources. Such a state of affairs is
hazardous on two fronts. It is potentially explosive, in that conflict
may flare out of control if the conflicting goals are inadequately
resolved. There is equally the possibility of stalemate, as when
irresistible forces collide with immovable objects. If those who find
themselves in such a situation are to maximize their goals, they
must engage in a little politicking: That is, they must trade off
their goals and resources. It can truly be said in such situations
that "politics is the art of the possible." We refer to such bargaining behavior as legislative in character, whatever its institutional
locus. Legislative behavior thus concerns primarily the resolution of
conflict in allocating goals and mobilizing resources.

Legislative institutions certainly have no monopoly of bargaining. As we have observed, bargaining is often found in relation-

---

*This comes very close to the hornbook definition of persuasion. One example of Presi-
dential persuasion is the so-called wage-price guidepost, which is described as a policy of
"education, persuasion, creation of a climate in the public mind designed to encourage
exercise of long-run self-interest. . . ."[18]

ships that are nominally hierarchical. The President, as we observed, finds himself enmeshed in a series of bargaining exchanges between and among his various constituencies and publics. At every level of the executive establishment, interagency relationships assume a bargaining character as the agencies maneuver for support in maximizing their goals. Not even the cloistered deliberations of courts are immune to bargaining.[19]

In our polity, however, legislatures are deliberately structured to promote bargaining relationships. Parity of legislators' resources is encouraged by the electoral process and by the rules under which the chambers operate. As we shall see in Chapter 2, the electoral process yields a collectivity of men and women who possess strikingly similar educational background, occupational status, and political experience. The great inequalities of social life are not reflected in the membership of Congress. Whether this result is desirable is, of course, open to debate. But the parity of members' resources unquestionably encourages bargaining relationships and discourages command relationships. Once duly seated, moreover, each member exercises the basic prerogatives of office—which include his vote, his committee assignments, and the assistance of his personal staff. By bringing these resources to bear upon the deliberations, "members in each body may make large individual contributions to public policy, although some members are more salient than others."[20]

The other condition of bargaining—disparity of goals—is also assured by the character of the legislative office. In the United States the electoral process is designed to produce a collectivity of men and women who answer to constituencies that are unique to them, not shared by other members. Their election or re-election is largely independent of the electoral fate of their colleagues. T. V. Smith, a scholar who served in the U.S. House of Representatives and the Illinois state legislature, put it this way:

> The legislature itself is a problem-solving place where men (and women) gather who owe little to one another but much to persons not there—persons, indeed, who seldom come there. We legislators owe only deference to one another, but both duty and victory to constituents back home.[21]

Members are expected to utilize their individual resources in order to maximize the goals held by discrete electorates.

Legislators' behavior on this score is reinforced not only by the structure of the body itself, but also by democratic tradition. The legislature is uniquely a collectivity of "fiduciary agents" (to use William Riker's suggestive concept) who act on behalf of their "principals," the voters. Since citizens cannot act for themselves, their interests must be maximized by their elected representatives. And because citizen interests are at stake, the fiduciary is obligated to strike the best bargains he can, in ways which might appear brash or uncivil if only his personal goals or interests were at issue. Thus, Riker concludes that "not only are fiduciary agents obligated to behave rationally but also the alternatives for maximizing and winning are greater for the agent than for the principal."[22] This fiduciary morality exists for legislators as a function of their elective status, regardless of the particular style or focus they select in performing these tasks. (In Chapter 4 alternative representational roles will be discussed.) To be certain, legislators may often be uncertain as to their principals' interests, or even desires; but what is clear is that legislators assume special duties and obligations from their fiduciary role, and that these in turn produce behaviors deliberately engaged in to fulfill the role.[23]

In the real world, legislative bodies approach but do not precisely reflect "perfect" conditions for bargaining. Not all goals are unshared, not all resources distributed equally. In any viable relationship at least *some* goals are shared by virtually all participants: Cohesion would be extremely tenuous if this were not the case. Stability in the American polity has been achieved, according to some commentators, because of an impressive consensus on fundamental goals, including the so-called "rules of the game."[24] However, even broadly shared goals may break down when applied to specific cases. Nor should the extent of consensus be overstated: On at least one occasion fundamental goals were contested by arms, and today a number of issues—Negro rights, welfare programs, the role of police, and involvement in foreign wars—expose deep and pervasive rifts in American society and in Congress.

In the face of large and significant disparities of goals, the best that can be said of the American polity is that it has generally kept the disparities at manageable levels. When goal conflicts have occurred, they have tended to be crosscutting rather than cumulative: Today's enemies may be tomorrow's allies when the focus or arena of conflict has shifted. Perhaps more importantly, abundance of national resources has tended to mute controversy by permitting a wide variety of individual and collective goals to be pursued concurrently. By definition, this enormously simplifies the task of bargaining among competing interests. In recent years, therefore, Congressional consensus has been solid on some domestic issues and many foreign policy issues.

The second condition for bargaining is never perfectly met, for the resources of legislators, or of other relevant actors, are rarely balanced equally. The formal powers of office are, to be sure, the same for all members; but, as any observer of Congress knows, some members are decidedly more equal than others. Even in a highly selective body such as Congress, personal talents are unevenly distributed among the members. Disparities in skills and information lead to the use of persuasion as an adjunct to bargaining and as the characteristic mode of legislative leadership. Consider Ralph K. Huitt's portrait of Lyndon B. Johnson, by all reckonings the most effective floor leader in the Senate's history. Johnson's success, Huitt observes, can be laid to his

> determination to persuade everyone who might be got to go in [Johnson's] way. The tactics ranged from the casual but pointed remark in his restless roaming of floor and cloakroom to the saturation treatment known as "Treatment A," in which the whole gamut of emotions—patriotism, loyalty, selfishness, fear, pride— might be played upon.[25]

Needless to add, formal positions within Congress, such as the party and committee hierarchies, confer on favored members disproportionate resources for restructuring the goals of the rank-and-file members. And in a parliamentary system where, as in the House of Commons, independent voting is discouraged by the use of potent sanctions, inequalities of resources are so great as to render bargaining very difficult indeed.

In Congress, however, bargaining is the rule rather than the exception, because every member has significant sanctions (resources) that can be brought to bear in the legislative arena. Indeed, no assessment of our national legislature is so frequently repeated as that which stresses its decentralized, collegial nature. Bargaining is perhaps more characteristic of the small Senate, and less so of the larger and more steeply structured House of Representatives. Yet both bodies are marked by a relatively nonhierarchical distribution of resources; and for this reason students have tended to define them as essentially bargaining institutions. As a sociologist, Robin Williams, has summed up the situation,

> Although there is a measure of hierarchy in the legislative branch—committee chairman, speakers and presiding officers, party whips, and so on—a popularly elected body is always a "college" of approximate equals who must reach their decisions by discussion, negotiation, "pressure," and various informal arrangements, rather than by a strict chain of command."[26]

Thus, we conclude that a legislature—while like all political structures displaying various forms of behaviors—is defined primarily by its character as a bargaining institution.

MODES OF BARGAINING

What is bargaining behavior, and what roles are likely to be associated with such behavior? Actually, bargaining is a generic term that refers to several related types of behaviors. In each case, an exchange of value occurs: Goals or resources pass from a bargainer's hands in return for other goals or resources that he values.[27] A simple typology of bargaining is presented in Table 1–3.

Table 1–3. Typology of Bargaining

Implicit	Explicit
Anticipated Reaction	Compromise
"Exchange of Trust"	Logrolling (simple, time, side-payments)

Bargaining may be worked out explicitly, or it may be implicit. An example of implicit bargaining occurs when a politician makes a speech or drafts a bill designed to elicit a certain reaction from others, even though no negotiation may have taken place—the so-called "law of anticipated reactions." Another example occurs when a legislator accepts the judgment of a better-informed colleague on a matter, expecting perhaps to have the situation reversed in future relationships ("exchanges of trust").

Explicit bargaining takes several forms. In a compromise, the actors agree to split their differences in some fashion—for example, when those favoring a $100-million aid program and those wanting no program at all are able to agree on a $50-million program; neither side fully achieves its goal, but both parties gain something. In logrolling, the parties trade off support so that each may gain its goal. In its most visible forms trading may be embodied in a something-for-everyone enactment; or in an agreement to support one measure now in exchange for support later on another bill (time logrolling); or in side payments, whereby support is exchanged for nonissue benefits. Such benefits may include assistance in campaigns, help in obtaining a desired committee assignment, a flattering invitation to a White House social affair, and many other items.

Logrolling, which is frequently given the opprobrious label "mutual back-scratching," is perhaps best exemplified by public works bills, whose many components permit a wide distribution of favors. Writing in 1885, Woodrow Wilson described the phenomenon as it operates in such porkbarrel measures:

> "Logrolling" is an exchange of favors. Representative A is very anxious to secure a grant for the clearing of a small watercourse in his district, and Representative B is equally solicitous about his plans for bringing money into the hands of the contractors of his own constituency, whilst Representative C comes from a seaport town whose modest harbor is neglected because of the treacherous bar across its mouth, and Representative D has been blamed for not bestirring himself more in the interest of schemes of improvement afoot amongst the enterprising citizens of his native place; so it is perfectly feasible for these gentlemen to put their heads together and confirm a mutual understanding that each will vote in Committee of the Whole for grants desired by the others in consideration of the promise that they will cry "aye" when his item comes on to be considered.[28]

Such practices, it hardly need be added, have not disappeared since Wilson's day.* Senator Paul H. Douglas' bill to aid areas of chronic unemployment underwent this treatment in 1956. Originally drafted to provide loans and grants to older industrialized regions, the bill met firm resistance from rural and southern legislators who, in the words of Senator J. William Fulbright (D-Ark.), opposed "special legislation for a few spots in Illinois, Pennsylvania and a few other places."[30] In return for their support, these legislators forced Douglas to extend his bill to include an equal

---

*Senator Paul H. Douglas once described a public works bill in the following language: "This bill is built up out of a whole system of mutual accommodations in which the favors are widely distributed, with the implicit promise that no one will kick over the applecart; that if Senators do not object to the bill as a whole, they will 'get theirs.' "[29]

amount of aid to rural areas of underemployment. Believing (rightly, as it turned out) that this change would water down his bill to the point of ineffectuality, Douglas referred ruefully to the new provisions as "Pass the biscuits, Pappy!"

To be sure, logrolling provides excellent fodder for criticism. But such behavior is essential if multiple, contested goals are to be realized. As we have seen, the legislator finds himself operating in an arena marked by imperfect integration of goals and resources. If outputs—in the form of authoritative goal allocations —are to be produced in such an arena, then bargaining must be resorted to. This bargaining is reflected in the substance of allocations and in many secondary attributes of the legislative process—delay, obfuscation, specialization, and other forms of integrative activity. Indeed, it is no exaggeration to say that such activity is a key feature of the Congressional way of life, one that extends far beyond the trading of votes. "The very essence of the legislative process," David Truman has remarked, "is the willingness to accept trading as a means."[31]*

If our characterization of the legislative way of life has any validity, it should be reflected in the self-images of legislators themselves. Available evidence indicates this to be the case. The "Senate folkways" described by Donald R. Matthews, for example, are precisely the kinds of norms one would expect to evolve among a group of fiduciary bargainers; and our knowledge of the House of Representatives suggests that such attitudes are equally prevalent there.[33] In Chapters 3 through 5 of this book we shall attempt to present and describe the role orientations of Representatives toward their tasks, their responsibilities as fiduciary agents, and their relationships with political parties and interest groups. The picture of the House member that emerges from these role orientations is, to a large measure, congruent with the conceptual viewpoint we have taken here. The substantive emphasis that our respondents gave to their tasks as Representatives, and the stylistic emphasis upon brokerage, are especially reflective of the extent to which the norms of fiduciary bargaining pervade Congress. In other respects the fit between concept and empirical finding is less perfect—reflecting, perhaps, the degree to which conditions for bargaining are not met, or the degree to which

---

*Matthews lists the reciprocity norm as one of the folkways of the Senate.[32]

legislators may misperceive the conditions under which they must work.

CONCLUSIONS

Thus far, the discussion has centered on a conceptual view of the legislator. First, the concept of system was examined as it applied to politics, stressing the functions that must be fulfilled by the political system if it is to survive the dual threats of external environment and internal dissension. The political system, or polity, is a social subsystem of enormous (and, in the view of most observers, increasing) importance, which performs goal attainment and other functions necessary for the continued existence of the larger society. One component of the polity is the legislature, which performs essential functions—primarily integration, but other tasks as well—for the polity. Starting from the inputs of the legislative system, we have been able to describe the modes of behavior that characterize the legislature as a collectivity of political agents.

If the discussion so far has been primarily conceptual, we will in subsequent pages attempt to give it, in Shakespeare's words, "a local habitation and a name." What has been attempted is a functional definition of the role of the legislator in the political system. This definition has been abstracted from empirical understandings on which students and observers generally agree. But little empirical evidence has been introduced to illustrate or explore the concepts themselves. It is to this task that subsequent chapters will be devoted.

In attempting to extend empirical understanding of the job of Congressmen, we will refer primarily to their *status* and *role* attributes. The term status refers to their position within the political (or social) system; the term role, to the normative requirements of their functioning within that status.[34] Specific measures of these attributes will be introduced and explained as the discussion proceeds.

CHAPTER 2

THE LEGISLATIVE CAREER

The framers of the Constitution displayed characteristic restraint in specifying qualifications for service in the House of Representatives. Age, citizenship, and residency are the only requirements mentioned in the Constitution. Beyond these, popular choice was to prevail. (The framers, of course, had other ideas concerning the upper house; but with the adoption of the Seventeenth Amendment, Senators too were chosen by popular election.)

What kinds of persons would be elected to the House? The author of *Federalist 57* answered:

> . . . every citizen whose merit may recommend him to the esteem and confidence of his country. No qualification of wealth, of birth, of religious faith, or of civil profession is permitted to fetter the judgment or disappoint the inclination of the people.[1]

The democratic norm of popular choice did not, of course, imply that legislators would be a cross-section of the citizenry at large. Electoral processes ought to yield that individual "whose merit may recommend him." Indeed, a crucial test of any political system was its capacity "to obtain for rulers men who possess most wisdom to discern, and most virtue to pursue, the common good of the society."[2] In meeting this objective, however, formal procedural safeguards alone would be of little avail.

For almost two centuries Congress has generally manifested the dual virtues that the framers claimed for it. Its doors remain open to a wide variety of men and women drawn from many walks of life. Yet in practice, recruitment standards are considerably more restrictive than the Constitutional requirements. Not all Americans are equally capable of running for (much less winning) public office; and for this reason, if for no other, those who serve in Congress differ in key respects from the electorate at large. While this fact of political life often dismays egalitarian democrats, it should come as no surprise to students of social systems. After all, it was Aristotle who first observed that elections are essentially oligarchic affairs.

Students of politics, whatever their value assumptions or research perspectives, are interested in the characteristics of persons in formal positions of influence. Marxists see in leaders' attributes a confirmation of their contention that the state is only the executive committee of the dominant economic class. Conservatives assess the same phenomena in light of their conviction that political domination by some form of elite is inevitable. It is important that backgrounds and careers of political elites be examined with precision and not merely with the curiosity of, say, a gossip columnist. "In studying legislative backgrounds," Roland Young wisely cautions, "a clear idea of the usefulness of the investigation for legislative theory is necessary if the study is not to end in the production of an unassimilated mass of facts."[3]*

Of course, legislators' attributes—their personalities, skills, experiences, and associations—constitute an important input of the legislative system of behavior.[5] These factors, that is to say, influence the goals and resources that legislators bring to the legislative arena; and their goals and resources in turn affect the success or failure of claimants outside that arena. This does not imply, of course, that a one-to-one relationship exists between a Congressman's background and, for instance, his vote on a given bill. "The politician-legislator," writes David B. Truman, "is not equivalent to the steel ball in a pinball game, bumping passively from post to post down an inclined plane."[6] Nonetheless, to dismiss background factors as irrelevant would be equally mistaken. As one perceptive student has asserted, "the study of a legislator from the Washington perspective alone is bound to be one-dimensional."[7]

---

*Along these same lines, Keller comments that ". . . the analysis of elites has suffered from . . . too much descriptive detail and too little systematic theoretical interpretation."[4]

But what is important to the following discussion is that the backgrounds and careers of legislators may influence the way they perceive their jobs. Our concern here is not primarily with specific policy outputs of the legislators, but rather with norms of behavior that they manifest. Unfortunately, direct relationships between legislators' backgrounds and their role perceptions have not been convincingly demonstrated. Indeed, it is often difficult to see what form such relationships would assume. For example, the predominance of lawyers in American legislatures is conceded by most observers to be a phenomenon of enormous significance. But exactly how does legal training or experience affect the lawyer-legislator's conception of his job? Does he transfer to the legislative arena mainly his experience in legal advocacy? Or is his skill at bargaining and negotiation more relevant? The answer is unclear, though students concur that the legal ethos pervades American legislative bodies.

As the ensuing discussion will attempt to make clear, it is probable that so-called background variables exert a subtle and indirect influence upon legislative role-taking. In the House of Representatives, for example, perhaps the strongest conclusion to be drawn from a study of background characteristics is that the recruitment process yields a remarkably homogeneous collectivity of men and women. The growth of House service as a distinctive career, moreover, has enhanced the saliency of the institution itself as a source of role expectations. Thus we are led to assume that the characteristics and shared experiences of the Congressional group affect the range and compatability of role perceptions, not to mention their saliency for members and the precision with which they are expressed. Therefore, as a background to our description of role-taking in the House, we shall want to develop broad hypotheses concerning the nature of the Congressional group.

In this chapter, three key background characteristics of Congressmen will be briefly examined: occupation, political experience, and geographic mobility. Additionally, the age and tenure of members will be studied for possible clues to the nature of the Congressional career. Finally evidence concerning the Congressional career will be sought in the length of legislative sessions—a factor that affects the level of commitment demanded of individual members. In examining all these factors, information from selected earlier Congresses will be employed along with information from contemporary Congressmen, in the hope of illuminating broad features of historical development.

LAWYERS AND OTHERS

"Occupationally," observes George B. Galloway, "the House of Representatives . . . has never been a mirror to the nation."[8] Although this proposition is indisputable, occupational data concerning legislators are not—for reasons to be explained presently —invariably reliable or easily assessed. However, our interviewees from the 88th Congress can be examined with some confidence, for particular care was exercised in obtaining career information beyond that usually found in published sources. Occupations of our random sample of eighty-seven members are shown in Table 2-1. (Explanation of sampling and data-gathering procedures is offered in Chapter 3 and in the Appendix.)

Slightly more than 60 per cent of the Congressmen had legal backgrounds. Not all of these actively practiced law, but all had completed their legal training. Nearly a third of the sample had experience in business or banking, although this constituted the primary occupation of no more than a quarter of the sample. Agriculture or farming was listed by 14 per cent, though often in combination with other occupations. Next, 9 per cent of the sample possessed experience in education (including teaching and school administration) and 9 per cent in other professions

Table 2–1. Occupational Backgrounds of
87 Members of the 88th Congress (1963–1964)

Occupation	Per cent of Members
Law	61%
Business and banking	31
Agriculture	14
Education	9
Other professional	9
Journalism	6
Other nonprofessional	6
Union official	2
Total	138%[a]

a Totals more than 100 per cent because many respondents listed more than one occupation. (For an explanation of sampling procedures, see Appendix.)

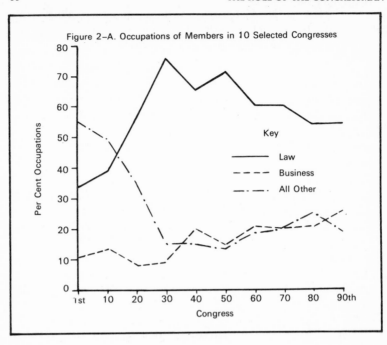

Figure 2–A. Occupations of Members in 10 Selected Congresses

Key

—————— Law

– – – – Business

– · – · – All Other

(including medicine, clergy, accounting, and engineering). And 6 per cent of the sample had journalistic experience.

With the possible exception of farming, the only occupations that could be classed as below middle-class status are in the final two categories. (Agriculture might be classed as low status, but in the case of Congressmen it typically involves ownership or proprietorship.) The nonprofessional category consists primarily of lower-status white-collar jobs in sales or clerical work. The two union officials in our sample began their careers as skilled laborers, but even they had spent most of their adult lives in white-collar jobs within their unions.

Have occupational patterns changed over time? In order to probe changes in the incidence of various occupations, the entire House membership for ten selected Congresses has been examined. The distribution of major occupations in these Congresses is shown in Figure 2-A. Though there is reason to believe that these data are broadly accurate, several caveats must be entered. First, occupational data are inherently difficult to categorize and evaluate. Not a few members engage in more than one occupation during their lifetimes, and the student must judge which occupation (or occupations) should be used for classification. A number of specialized occupations, too, present problems of categorization. These problems are probably endemic to any study of occupations, and the best that can be said is that the student must accept the data in full awareness of their shortcomings. Second, published biographical materials, especially for the earlier Congresses, are incomplete. Finally, however, there is the possibility that the Congresses selected for analysis were atypical of the periods they represent. Fortunately, in a few instances the figures can be compared with available information for other Congresses of the same period. In certain other cases, inconsistencies in the data lead to suggestive hypotheses concerning short-term changes in Congressional personnel.*

"Ours is a government of lawyers and not of men," the waggish saying goes. As Figure 2–A shows, the legal profession has almost always been the dominant occupational background for members of the House of Representatives. A similar situation exists in the Senate, where Matthews found that "no other occupational group even approaches the lawyers' record."[9] The lawyer's importance to the political life of the United States can hardly be overstated; and although the law has also been a significant source of political leaders in other western democracies, nowhere has it attained the prominence it has enjoyed in this country.[10] Lawyers also abound among executives at the national level—including Presidents, Vice Presidents, and Cabinet members[11]—and among state Governors (though with important re-

---

*Unless otherwise noted, historical data presented in this chapter are drawn from analysis of the members of the House in the 1st and 10th Congresses and every tenth succeeding Congress, ending with the 90th. The primary source of information concerning members was the *Biographical Directory of the American Congress, 1774–1961* (Washington, D. C.: U.S. Government Printing Office, 1961). For recent Congresses this material was supplemented by *Congressional Directories* and *Who's Who in America*. Figures represent the members' primary occupations before election to office. When a member engaged in more than one occupation, the occupation chosen was the one at which he was employed for the longest period of time, or in case of simultaneous employment the one judged to have taken the major portion of his time. In a few cases where no decision could be reached, more than one occupation was allowed. Categories were: law; business (including banking); public service (including military, government, or civil service, and public or elective positions where there was no evidence of other occupation); agriculture; labor (including union leadership); education; clergy; journalism; medicine; and other (including other professions, clerical work, and women who gained office upon the death of their husbands).

gional variations).[12] A similar situation is found in state legislatures, which, however, show marked regional variation and generally appear to have fewer lawyers than Congress.[13] Lasswell and McDougal have truly observed that, "For better or worse our decision-makers and our lawyers are bound together in a relation of dependence or of identification."[14]

For the House of Representatives, as for other political collectivities, then, a "professional convergence" of law and politics exists.[15] Several reasons for this convergence can be enumerated. The lawyer typically enjoys what is termed "job dispensability," because he can move readily in and out of his job without jeopardizing his career. Such mobility would be impossible in many other professions, like medicine, where a temporary respite can ruin a career.[16] Nor is it usually the case with the corporate businessman, for whom a temporary leave of absence could mean exclusion from the ladder of advancement. The lawyer, however, may find a foray into politics to his professional advantage, and in fact such a course is considered an important method of ethical advertising. Thus, a person contemplating a political career may enter law to further his goal. (The lawyer-politician, incidentally, tends to enter politics earlier than his nonlawyer colleagues.)[17] Finally, the profession of law emphasizes personal skills of verbalization, advocacy, or negotiation, which are useful in seeking and holding public office. For these and other reasons, law and politics are in our society closely intertwined.

Business is the next most prevalent occupation, though it has never been more than a distant second to law. The trend for businessmen in Congress has been decidedly bullish both in absolute numbers and precentages. In the 90th Congress (1967–1968) more than one of every four Representatives came from a business background.

Aside from law and business, no other occupational category has since the 60th Congress (1907–1909) accounted for more than 6 per cent of the membership. Occupations other than law or business appear to have been heavily represented in the three earliest Congresses, partly because of a prevalence of so-called "public service" occupations—a category that is, especially in the case of early members, unsatisfactorily vague. Taken together, all of the remaining occupations (that is, excluding law and business) have equalled or exceeded the number of businessmen in only two of the six selected Congresses since the Civil War. In the 90th Congress, for example, 26 per cent of the members claimed backgrounds in business, while 20 per cent represented all the remaining occupations.

Needless to say, the occupations that make up by far the largest sector of the nation's labor force have been drastically underrepresented in Congress. Agriculture, for example, claimed a high of 14 per cent of the members of the 10th Congress (1807-1809), but since the 30th Congress (1847-1849) it has produced no more than 6 per cent of the membership of the Congresses examined. Other occupational groupings—education, journalism, medicine, and the clergy—have been represented steadily though in small numbers. Few if any of these occupations, it should be remembered, would be considered low- or even middle-status. And countless other low-status occupations—including farm labor, the service trades, manual and skilled labor, and domestic service—have been virtually unknown in the halls of Congress.[18]

The occupational mixture in the House is not unchanging. Nor should the predominance of lawyer-legislators be considered inevitable. As Figure 2-A reveals, nonlegal occupations actually predominated in the 1st and 10th Congresses. Only a third of the members of the First Congress (1789-1791) were lawyers. Legal training quickly became the norm, however: The proportion of lawyers in the House rose to 38 per cent in the 10th Congress (1807-1809) and 51 per cent in the 9th and 13th Congresses combined (1805-1807 and 1813-1815).[19]* For the remainder of the nineteenth century lawyers made up well over 60 per cent of the House, reaching a highwater mark (for the Congresses examined) of 76 per cent in the 30th Congress (1847-1849).† In the twentieth century the proportion of lawyers in the House has actually declined, while their share of the civilian labor force has remained relatively constant at .3 per cent. In Congresses since World War II, lawyers have comprised slightly more than half of the total membership.

Shifts in the occupational mixture within the House are in large part traceable to broad trends of economic and social growth. A regional summary of occupational backgrounds—law, business,

---

*The proportion of lawyers rose by 13.2 per cent between the 9th and 13th Congresses.
†In the 29th Congress (1845-1847) the proportion was 72 per cent; in the 54th (1895-1897), 67 per cent.[20]

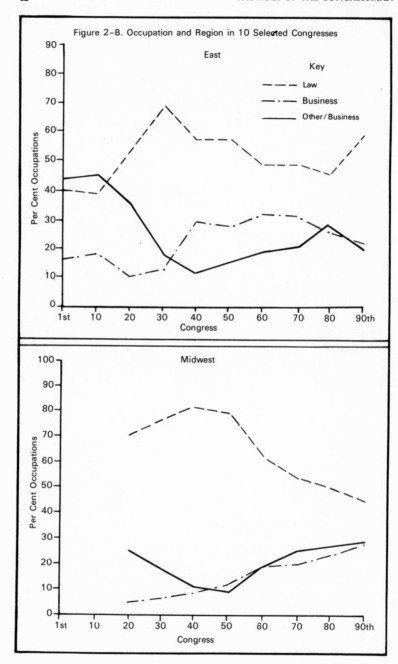

Figure 2-B. Occupation and Region in 10 Selected Congresses

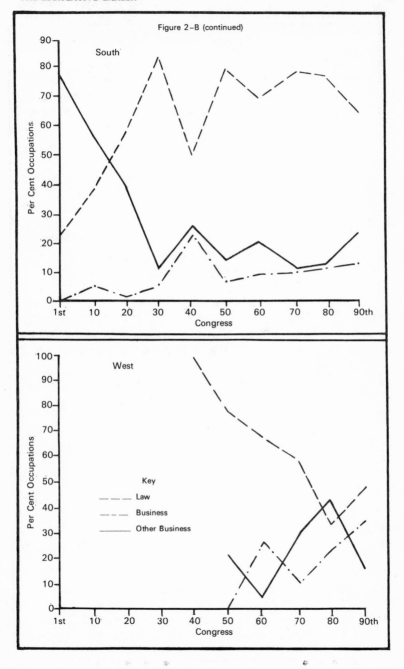

Figure 2–B (continued)

and all others—is presented in Figure 2-B.* Of the four regions, the East shows the most stable and balanced occupational pattern. A consistently large proportion of eastern Congressmen have been businessmen (since the Civil War, between 23 and 32 per cent), a fact which probably reflects the importance of business and financial enterprise to the area. And while lawyers have dominated most eastern delegations, they have done so to a lesser extent than in other areas of the country. Occupationally, eastern Congressmen appear to reflect a relatively developed and stable society with a broad occupational base.

The newer regions of the country have manifested an evolution in the direction of the East's occupational mixture. This evolution has been much more rapid in the newer frontier region of the West than in the older frontier of the Midwest—a reflection, no doubt, of accelerating nationalization in economic development and diversification. In both frontier regions (whose Congressional delegations can be traced almost from their beginnings), the legal profession virtually monopolized early Congressional delegations but has dropped off markedly during the present century. In the Midwest there was relative stability in the occupational backgrounds of members throughout the nineteenth century; and in the present century the decline of law and commensurate rise of business have been gradual.

No such stability is found among western delegations. The proportion of lawyers from the West has fallen precipitously ever since the region was first represented in Washington: Only 33 per cent of western members in the 80th Congress and 49 per cent in the 90th Congress were lawyers. Similarly, business and other occupations have grown dramatically in the West, compared with their more gradual growth in the Midwest. In turn, nonlaw occupations have enjoyed somewhat greater growth in the Midwest than in the East or South. Doubtless a variety of social, economic, and political factors are associated with the occupational bases of political leadership; but present findings seem

*In this chapter and the remainder of the book, geographic regions are defined as follows: East (Me., N. H., Vt., Mass., R. I., Conn., N. Y., N. J., Penna., Del., Md., W. Va.); South (Ky., Tenn., Ala., Ga., N. C., S. C., Va., Fla., Tex., La., Okla., Miss., Ark.); Midwest (Mich., Minn., Wis., Mo., Ohio, Ia., Neb., Kan., Ill., Ind., S. D., N. D.); West (Ida., Utah, Mont., Haw., Calif., Ariz., Alaska, N. Mex., Wyo., Wash., Ore., Nev., Colo.).

to suggest a generalized linkage of economic development to the occupational mixture of Congressional delegations.

The South provides a fascinating variation on this theme. As Figure 2–B shows, Southerners in the first three Congresses studied were strongly representative of "other" occupations—primarily agriculture. As the nineteenth century progressed, however, the dominance of the legal profession became almost complete. Indeed, law and politics have been more intimately linked in the South than in any other region.

Some of the roots of this phenomenon are found in the nature of southern society. It is commonly observed that the "old South" was an underdeveloped region, mainly rural and agricultural; this image, redolent of magnolia blossoms and cotton fields, has given way rapidly to that of the industrialized "new South." The relatively limited occupational mixture of past southern delegations, and the great preponderance of legal backgrounds, may have been a function of an economy that offered few attractive career alternatives for ambitious young men. Accordingly, it could be predicted that as the region advances in economic activity and diversity, the proportion of lawyer-Congressmen will decline as business and other occupations increase. Figures for the 90th Congress indicate that this trend is well on its way.

The unique occupational pattern in the South also has a partisan dimension. Southern Democrats have been rather consistently the most lawyer-dominated grouping in the House, the proportion of lawyers ranging between 70 and 90 per cent for all the Congresses examined. In contrast, occupational ratios in the Republican party have been quite erratic. With this fact in mind, we can return to some of the interesting features of Figure 2–B.

In the 40th Congress (1867–1869) the disfranchisement of Confederate sympathizers and the accompanying influx of carpetbaggers had the effect of upsetting the normal occupational mixture. Lawyers constituted only half of the southern delegation, with those from business or other occupations making up the remainder. This turn of events accompanied a reshuffling of party ratios: Of the twenty-seven nonlawyer southerners in the 40th Congress, 85 per cent were Republican. More recently, the proportion of southern lawyers dipped significantly between the 80th (1945–1946) and 90th (1967–1968) Congresses, while businessmen showed a comparable increase. A major factor in this change was the increasing number of southern Republican Congressmen: from 6 per cent to 24 per cent of the region's contingent during this twenty-year period. (Among southern Republicans in the 90th Congress, 41 per cent were businessmen and 45 per cent lawyers; in contrast, 18 per cent of the Democrats were businessmen and 71 per cent lawyers.)

Thus, the traditional dominance of the legal profession in the South is closely associated with Democratic hegemony. As the Republican party gains firmer footholds in the region, the number of lawyers may decline still further, resembling more closely the ratio in other regions. Yet economic changes in the South—which have no doubt fostered southern Republicanism as well as increased representation of businessmen—have also had an impact on the Democratic party: In the 90th Congress business backgrounds among southern Democratic Congressmen were at the highest level in history—nearly two thirds larger than in any sampled Congress since Reconstruction.

Interparty occupational differences in the South account for much of the variation between the occupational bases of Democrats and Republicans in the House. Nationally, divergencies between the parties are not great: In both parties legal backgrounds have declined and business backgrounds risen since the mid-nineteenth-century. One national variation is that more lawyers, and fewer businessmen and representatives of other occupations, are found in Democratic ranks than in Republican, for the Congresses analyzed. Among Republicans, also, there has been a more rapid (though erratic) decline of lawyers and rise of businessmen.

Outside the South, the parties are hardly distinguishable in terms of broadly defined occupations. This point can be demonstrated by omitting the South and presenting data for the remainder of the country, as in Figure 2–C. Here we see strikingly revealed the bipartisan character of occupational trends in House membership. Though in recent times more Republican than Democratic Congressmen have been recruited from the business world, this has not always been the case. The Democrats had a larger proportion of businessmen than the Republicans in the pre-Depression 70th Congress, and for the other Congresses examined the interparty differences are not large. The long-term decline of law, coupled with a rise of business (and of other occupations), is common to both parties.

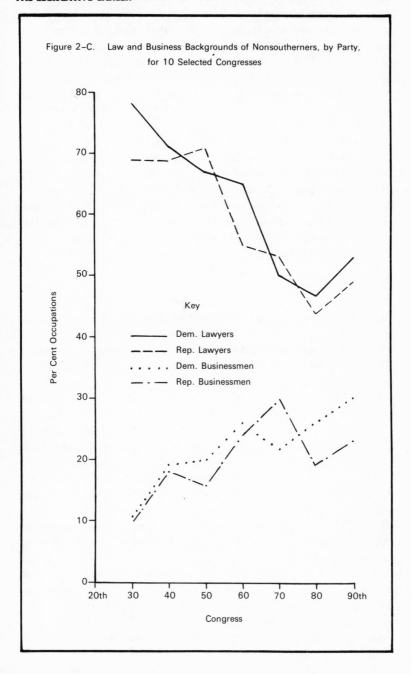

Figure 2–C.   Law and Business Backgrounds of Nonsoutherners, by Party, for 10 Selected Congresses

These gross occupational figures no doubt hide certain subtle yet important differences in the two parties' bases of recruitment. First, there could be significant interparty variations in "other" occupations. Though a few such variations do appear, they do not seem significant taken as a whole. A more forceful objection is that the parties recruit essentially different kinds of persons within the same broad categories of law and business. Among Senators of the 1947–1957 period, Donald R. Matthews found that Democratic businessmen were largely merchants, contractors, oil and gas producers, and insurance and real estate men; Republicans, on the other hand, tended to be publishers and manufacturing executives. Matthews inferred that "in the Senate, Democratic and Republican businessmen tend to be different."[21] The same is probably true within the legal fraternity. There is a vast difference, for example, between a county-seat lawyer (southern Democrat) and a corporate lawyer (northern Republican).

Many social theorists suggest the likelihood of increasing specialization of elite career patterns, and increasing rigidity of career ladders within each elite. This phenomenon would presumably be accompanied by the prevalence of a very few occupations—increasingly, to the virtual exclusion of others—and by ever more stable levels of representation for each occupational category. These latter assumptions, it now appears, are not necessarily borne out. To be sure, two occupations—business and especially law—have been prevalent throughout the history of Congress. But the relative position of the two has changed. Indeed, the decline of law and the rise of business has been a steady phenomenon since the late nineteenth century. Other occupations, too, have been appearing with somewhat greater frequency. (Eighty-eight per cent of the Congressmen with labor backgrounds, for example, appear in the last three Congresses examined.) Evolution in the occupational make-up of Congress does not seem to have come to a halt. Indeed, if the decline in legal backgrounds may be taken as a significant trend, the data suggest a certain widening of the occupational base of recruitment.

At least one finding, moreover, points to a continuation of this trend. As has been pointed out, the prevalence of lawyer-Congressmen is due in some part to the special place of the lawyer in less developed regions of the country—the Midwest, West, and South, in that order. If these regions continue to increase their resemblance to the urbanized, industrialized, and economically diversified East, a further "levelling downward" in the position of the legal fraternity in the halls of Congress may occur. Whether this development will eventually produce a kind of occupational equilibrium—reflecting a rigidified pre-Congressional career pattern—can only be guessed at. This could well be the case, if theory on the matter is of any validity. In any event, occupations themselves are not the sole indicators, and perhaps not the crucial ones, of the evolving Congressional career pattern. Thus, we must examine other aspects of Congressional careers.

THE PROFESSIONAL POLITICIANS

Perhaps a more important feature of the pre-Congressional career is the member's apprenticeship in local and state politics, either holding public office or working for his party. Persons in high public office tend to be veteran political activists by the time they gain election. The typical United States Senator, Matthews found, began his political career early—usually just after graduating from college—and by the time he was elected to the Senate had held three offices and spent half his adult life (about ten years) in public life.[22] In the House of Representatives, too, political careerism is the rule rather than the exception. From its beginnings the House has been a collectivity of professionals. In the 1st Congress, at least 25 of the 26 Senators and 52 of the 65 Representatives had served either in the Constitutional Convention, the Continental Congress, a state legislature, or a state constitutional convention.[23] Since that time, Galloway estimated, at least a third of all Representatives have served in state legislatures before coming to Washington. At least 17 Congressmen have been former Governors of their states, while more than 50 sat previously in the United States Senate. One former President, John Quincy Adams, crowned his illustrious career by serving seventeen years in the House. "My election as President was not half so gratifying to my inmost soul," he said of his election by the people of Quincy, Massachusetts.[24]

Information on the prior political careers of Congressmen is bound to be unsatisfactory as long as published sources must be relied upon. In our survey of eighty-seven members of the 88th Congress, however, published biographies were supplemented with material gathered in questionnaires. The figures, presented in Table 2-2, strikingly confirm the extensive apprenticeship of House members. Only 6 per cent of the respondents had no discernible prior political experience. This figure may if anything be on the conservative side, since it includes members for whom no information could be obtained as well as those who clearly lacked political experience. Members in the sample held an average of 2.2 positions prior to their election to Congress. Though the extent of apprenticeship ranged widely, fully three quarters of the members were veterans of political party work at the state or local levels, and 47 per cent had served in a state legislature. The one member who had served as Governor of his small state also had experience in virtually every other type of state and local activity.

In number of prior offices held, our sample of Representatives revealed slightly less experience than the Senators studied by Matthews. Senators during the period 1947 to 1957 held an average of 3 public (*i.e.*, governmental) positions before their election to the Senate, while our Representatives had served in an average of 2.2 posts—including volunteer party jobs as well as public offices. This disparity is understandable, if only because the

Table 2–2. Prior Political Experience of 87 Members of the House (88th Congress)

Type of Experience	Per cent of Members
State or local party position	75%
State legislature	47
City or county law enforcement	26
City or county elective position	12
City or county judicial position	12
State appointive position	9
National party position	9
Other city or local position[a]	8
Other federal position[b]	8
Federal law enforcement position	6
State elective position	1
No previous political experience	6
Total	218%[c]

a Includes appointive boards, commissions, etc.
b Includes executive, civil service, and legislative staff.
c Totals more than 100 per cent because members averaged 2.2 positions apiece.

House is for some politicians one step in a career ladder leading to the Senate. In recent decades, in fact, slightly more than a fourth of all Senators have first served in the House.[25] Thus, Senators as a group would be expected to exhibit greater political experience than Representatives.

Republicans and Democrats showed many similarities and a few differences in patterns of experience. In both parties, virtually the same proportion of members (94 per cent) possessed discernible political experience, again including party work as well as public office. And the same proportion (83 per cent) had held *public* office prior to their election. In variety of experience, Republicans in our sample came out slightly ahead of their Democratic colleagues. Republicans appeared in an average of 2.4 categories, while Democrats averaged 2.1 categories. The pattern of experience also differed somewhat between the parties. Democrats were more likely than Republicans to have served in a state legislature (53 per cent to 38 per cent); but Republicans led in holding law enforcement posts (44 to 25 per cent). Interestingly, political party service figured equally in the two parties.

An examination of historical trends in political apprenticeship is essential for describing the development of the pre-Congressional career. Unfortunately, the available data may never be entirely adequate to our needs. Biographical materials, rarely satisfactory (especially for more obscure members), are even less so in documenting political experience. Even if public officeholding can be verified, partisan experience is usually neglected by biographies, existing (if at all) in countless and irretrievable local, county, and state records. Hence, only very tentative statements can be ventured concerning this crucial dimension of the political career. From our study of ten selected Congresses it is possible, however, to indicate the over-all frequency of prior public officeholding among Congressmen. Included in our analysis were all recorded public offices held by the members.

With two exceptions, approximately 85 to 90 per cent of the members of the Congresses examined had held public office before their election to the House. Prior political experience has been high in both political parties throughout their history. During the twentieth century, however, slightly more Democrats than Republicans have manifested such experience.

In recent Congresses, prior formal officeholding seems to have decreased perceptibly within both parties. Whether this development is significant in magnitude, the present data do not permit us to say with confidence. Such a trend would seem inconsistent with the notion that political careers ought to become more structured with time—a phenomenon that would presumably be reflected in increased prior officeholding. Two possible explanations, however, suggest themselves. First, the data unquestionably underestimate the many informal and volunteer jobs, performed typically in local or state political party organizations. More thorough examination of the careers of members of the 88th Congress (Table 2-2) and the 90th Congress indicates that such posts continue to figure importantly in the backgrounds of three quarters or more of the members. Though no valid comparisons can be made with earlier Congresses, this fact itself certainly suggests no diminution of political careerism. Secondly, even if one assumes a decline in *public* officeholding, this decline could merely mean that the career ladder to Congress has become more distinct from career ladders to other public offices. One might hypothesize that politicians attracted to national office now follow a career pattern which, to a greater extent than formerly, bypasses local and state offices.

The two Congresses that stand as exceptions to these generalizations are instructive, as exceptions often are. The 1st Congress deviated from the "normal" level in that virtually all (97 per cent) of its members had previous experience in public life. In these terms at least, the initial Congress was perhaps the most "professional" group ever to convene as our national legislature. Virtually all of the men who convened in New York in 1789 had participated in the Constitutional Convention, the Continental or Confederation Congresses, or in various local and state councils. Their election to the Congress under the new Constitution was a natural outgrowth of earlier involvement in the affairs of the new nation. Perhaps at no point in our history was the political elite so small in absolute numbers, or so closely bound by common experience. As the period of revolution and Constitution-making ended and the affairs of the new nation settled into more stable patterns, this aging revolutionary elite probably fell away quite rapidly. Certainly there is little evidence that it extended very far into the first decade of the nineteenth century.[26]

Interestingly, this phenomenon was repeated in the two frontier regions, the Midwest and West, during their earliest years of representation on Capitol Hill. In each case, virtually every one of the few Representatives chosen from these new regions had discernible political experience prior to election. In each case, too, the proportion of politically experienced members soon dropped to "normal" levels, just as it had in the original states of the East and South after 1789. Although fuller examination would be required to confirm this finding, it appears that new regions displayed what might be called a "Founding Fathers syndrome" in selecting their early Representatives. Those chosen to represent a locality possessed wide experience in the political affairs of the territory—having usually served in the territorial legislature, or in appointed office, or in the state constitutional convention. Election to Congress was a logical capstone, perhaps even a reward, for their efforts. As the years passed, these founders disappeared from the scene, and the offices became accessible to persons with other backgrounds.

A second exception of sorts was the 80th Congress (1947–1948), in which only about 82 per cent of the members had previous political experience, by our definition. This unusually low proportion can be explained only partly by any long-range decline in prior officeholding. It so happens that the 80th Congress also had an unusually large number of freshman members—24 per cent, as opposed to the 13 to 17 per cent common for Congresses of the period. The large number of newcomers suggests an explanation for the drop in careerism among the members of that Congress. Of those freshmen lacking previous political experience, a disproportionate number were returning World War II veterans. For this limited period of time at least, war service apparently served for some aspirants as a substitute for political apprenticeship. It is noteworthy that both Richard M. Nixon and John F. Kennedy entered the 80th Congress in just this manner. Although this historical circumstance was transitory, a little reflection will suggest other accomplishments that may similarly substitute for political apprenticeship—including movie stardom, athletic prowess, service as an astronaut, and radio or television exposure of some sort. Nor is it likely that such alternative paths to public office will be diminished, given the increasing capacity of communications media to create celebrities.

A final evidence of the relative extent of the pre-Congressional career is the age of members upon their first election to the House. There are at least two reasons for thinking that age level might be on the upswing. First, our era is marked by generally increasing life expectancy and lengthening educational or professional preparation. Second, if the political career has become more structured with time, this development would likely be reflected in a lengthening period of preparation for high public office. For these reasons at least, it might be expected that entry into the House would be increasingly restricted to more mature persons.

This is not the case, as will be seen from Figure 2-E below. Although freshman Congressmen are considerably above the median age for the population at large, they do not appear to be getting older. In recent years, in fact, the general trend has been toward younger first-term Congressmen. Figure 2-E reveals considerable fluctuation in the age of first-termers, a phenomenon no doubt related to broader demographic changes in the population. But since the mid-nineteenth-century, no trend toward older first-term Congressmen has occurred.

In summary, available information on the political careers of members of Congress indicates that these men and women are political professionals. Probably well over 90 per cent of the members of any contemporary Congress have served apprenticeship in some segment of our political life. Important variations in political career patterns no doubt exist between the parties and among the various states and regions; our general knowledge of political careers certainly indicates this to be the case.[27] Present data are inadequate for full exploration of these variations, though it has been noted that Democratic Congressmen seem slightly more likely than Republicans to have held prior office. The data also indicate a slight over-all diminution of prior *public* officeholding, though there is no evidence that this extends to *partisan* officeholding. Upon occasion, aspirants can substitute nonpolitical accomplishment—*e.g.,* military service—for the normal route of political apprenticeship. But all in all, the office of Representative has been and continues to be reserved for those who have proved themselves in other political assignments.

LOCAL BOYS MAKE GOOD

Localism is one of the strongest and most inviolable norms in

American electoral politics. In this respect, our political tradition resembles the French and differs from the British. One of the few Constitutional qualifications for Representatives is that they be "inhabitants" of the state from which they were elected. This provision was deliberate. Members of the lower house, explained the author of *Federalist 56*, will carry to the seat of government ". . . a considerable knowledge of [state] laws, and a local knowledge of their respective districts."[28] This norm appeared in electoral behavior as early as 1789 and remains firmly fixed in the minds of voters.[29] Indeed, *de facto* standards are somewhat more stringent than the letter of the Constitution: Although the term "inhabitant" can be interpreted loosely, voter feeling against carpetbagging candidates usually works to restrict Congressional office to those with long and intimate association with the locale.

Most Congressmen therefore boast long and active association with their district before election. This fact constitutes an important dimension of apprenticeship, and can be bypassed only with difficulty. It is instructive to examine further this aspect of the pre-Congressional career. First, what trends can be discerned over a period of time in the geographic origins of Congressmen? Another question concerns the relationships of Congressmen to members of other political or nonpolitical elite groupings. Members of Congress are often criticized for their localism; and some political scientists have suggested that some of Congress' conflicts with other institutions can be traced to the narrower geographic backgrounds of its members.[30] In analyzing our ten selected Congresses, a simple test of geographic mobility was employed: whether the member was born in the state from which he was elected. Admittedly a crude definition of mobility, it is nonetheless indicative of the generalized phenomenon. While it understates mobility within the borders of a single state, it overstates interstate movement that occurs early in the member's life.

When geographic mobility, thus defined, is plotted for the membership of the ten selected Congresses, the results are as in Figure 2–D. The mobility levels represented in Congress follow a convex curve. Slightly more than one quarter of the members of the 1st and 10th Congresses were born in a state other than the one from which they were elected; the same was true in the two most recent Congresses studied, the 80th and 90th. However, Congressmen became increasingly mobile as the nineteenth century progressed, until in the 40th Congress slightly more than half the legislators were born in another state. That Congress included a large number of carpetbag Republicans in the South (26 of the 38 southern Republicans were born out of state, compared with 2 of the 12 southern Republicans twenty years later); but the trend was not confined to that region. By the 50th Congress (1887–1889) the number of geographically mobile legislators was on the downswing.

The major factor associated with the increase in geographic mobility was apparently the addition of new states (See Figure 2–D). As part of the frontier, these states at first had a relatively small native-born population. As time passed the number of native citizens grew; but because of continued migration into the area the proportion of native-born rose more slowly. Thus, the proportion of non-native-born Congressmen declined gradually in the newer regions. During the early years of a state's representation in Congress, the entire delegation was composed of men born elsewhere. Native-born political aspirants soon appeared, however, and as the region matured they came to dominate its delegations. Both the West and the Midwest show this predictable and steady downward trend. By the late 1960's, only in the far West was a large portion (almost half) of Congressmen born elsewhere. In contrast, the East has shown remarkable consistency over the 180-year period. The South is notable mainly for the carpetbag 40th Congress, in which fully two thirds of its Congressmen were born out of state. During the twentieth century the South has elected the most "localist" members, though a slight upturn of mobility in the 90th Congress reflects the renaissance of the Republican party, which recruits proportionately more of its leadership from newcomers to that region.

A comparison of geographic mobility within the two parties reveals that significantly more Republican Congressmen have been born out of state (a difference which, incidentally, failed to materialize in the 90th Congress). This difference held for all regions and virtually all occupational categories. Except in the South, where the difference may be related to the slightly higher numbers of businessmen recruited by the Republicans, the available data cast no further light on this partisan distinction. Perhaps the answer lies again in the fact that the two parties recruit from different strata within the same professions. Matthews found,

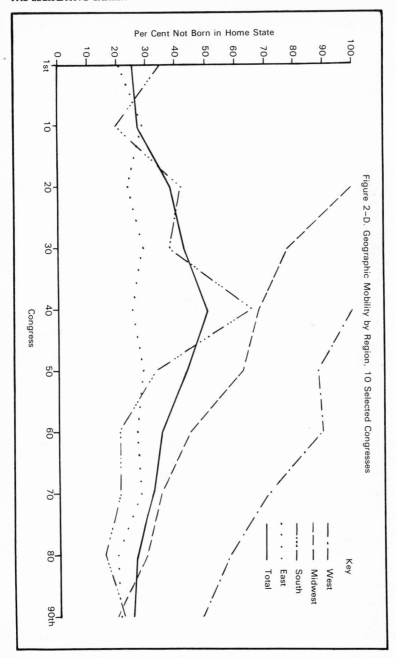

Figure 2–D. Geographic Mobility by Region, 10 Selected Congresses

Table 2–3. Geographic Mobility of Selected National Leaders[a]

Mobility	Cong'l. Ldrs. (1963)	Admin. Ldrs. (1963)	Pol. Execs. (1959)	Bsns. Ldrs. (1952)	Population at Large (1960)
None	37%	11%	14%	40%	70%
Intrastate	40	19			
Interstate, intraregion	5	9	10	15	12
Inter-region	19	61	73	45	14
International	0	0	3	0	4

a First four columns from Huntington, *op. cit.,* p. 13. Final column from U.S. Bureau of the Census, *Historical Statistics of the United States, Colonial Times to 1957: Continuation and Revisions to 1963* (Washington: U.S. Government Printing Office, 1963), p. 8.

as noted earlier, that Democratic lawyer-Senators tended to come from smaller law firms than Republicans; and that Democratic businessmen were more likely to be local merchants or entrepreneurs, whereas Republicans were more frequently corporate executives.[31] Assuming the same pattern in the House of Representatives, it seems reasonable to infer that Republican members are drawn from more mobile strata than are Democrats, even within the very same occupational groupings.

Are members of Congress more local in their backgrounds than other groupings in our society? There is no simple answer to this question. In comparison with the entire adult population, Congressmen seem neither more nor less mobile. (See Table 2–3.) However, when compared with the several rival elite groupings, Congressmen do appear much more local in their backgrounds. A sketchy comparison of several national leadership groups from material gathered by Huntington is presented in Table 2–3. The figures are open to some question because only Congressional leaders, not the whole membership, were analyzed. (It must be remembered that Congressional leaders are disproportionately southern, and that southerners in turn are disproportionately localist in background.) These Congressional leaders, however, enjoy much less geographic mobility than groupings of Cabinet members, sub-Cabinet federal political executives, and business leaders.

It can be argued that the local backgrounds of Congressmen explain some of the conflict between the national legislature and other elite subsystems. Yet localism should not be too quickly interpreted as parochialism, for the occupational and educational backgrounds of Representatives unquestionably render them more cosmopolitan than the vast majority of their constituents. Nor do local backgrounds necessarily lead members to assume localist roles of behavior. Indeed, one finding of the present study is that many members who (like the archetypical southerner) seem to the outside observer to have the narrowest outlook are in fact the least locally oriented. But this argument leads us beyond the present concerns.[32]

Data concerning the geographic mobility of Congressmen, then, confirm the common observation that the typical Congressional background encompasses a relatively narrow geographic area. Both the expectations of voters and the recruitment habits of local parties encourage this attribute. Historically, levels of mobility in Congress have varied largely because of the addition of new frontier states. One relatively consistent party difference also appears, in that Democrats tend to recruit from among less mobile persons, even within the same profession. Finally, Congressmen are about as mobile as the general public but much less so than other elite groupings.

THE WASHINGTON CAREERS

Considered collectively, members of Congress constitute a very privileged and homogeneous group of men and women. The characteristics we have discussed thus far in this chapter help to clarify the status of Congressmen. The fact that most legislators possess similar occupational training, perspectives, and status level; that they share a localized background that democratic norms insist should be brought to bear in decision-making; and that they share the camaraderie of the professional political fraternity —these attributes, and others as well, help to describe Congress as a group. More importantly for the present analysis, such factors may have an impact upon the notions that members develop concerning their jobs. The fact that many of these attributes are shared, moreover, enhances the likelihood that occupants of this institutional position will possess similar, or at least complementary, role perceptions.

To these background characteristics must be added a quite

different phenomenon—the shared Washington experience. Working in fragmented and largely unco-ordinated fashion, the electoral process yields a collectivity of men and women who possess striking similarities among their differences. If the collectivity is to function successfully, backgrounds and talents of members must somehow mesh into an institutional system that can cope with a complex environment and mounting quantities of legislative business. As Congress has matured, it has therefore evolved its own hierarchies of leadership, historic traditions, and accepted patterns of behavior (or folkways).[33] Thus the members, once settled in Washington, find themselves part of an ongoing group whose shared experiences supplement the experiences of individual members in determining role expectations. And every evidence indicates that this group is an ever more pervasive influence upon members of Congress.

Whatever the members' prior careers, they are apt to make a career out of legislative office. Tenure in office has increased steadily as the political system has matured. In the 1st Congress, of course, all members started afresh—though, as we noted, many had already served in earlier national legislative bodies. In the nineteenth century, the average tenure of Congressmen usually ranged from 2 to 2.5 terms. At the turn of the twentieth century, the average passed 3 terms; and by the 90th Congress, the average member had served no less than 5.5 terms—or approximately 11 years.[34]

This rise in Congressional tenure has added to the professionalism of the body in a second way: Fewer members of any given Congress are newcomers to Capitol Hill. In the nineteenth century it was not uncommon for half of the members of the House to be newcomers to their posts. Reflecting on the Jeffersonian period, James S. Young found that on the average, the biennial turnover (for the first forty years of the nation) was 41.5 per cent of total membership.[35] In the mid-twentieth-century, however, a turnover rate of between 15 and 20 per cent is typical.[36] Of those interviewed in our sample of eighty-seven members of the 88th Congress (1963–1964), 19 per cent were freshmen (compared to 15.2 per cent of the entire membership).

No clearer testimony to the increasing professionalization of the House exists than the lengthening of members' tenure. Nelson W. Polsby has pointed out that this development has been accompanied by a proliferation of career opportunities within the House, and by lengthening apprenticeship for House leadership posts.[37] Whether the framers of the Constitution anticipated this development is not known. On the one hand, they viewed frequent turnover in office as the most efficacious means of insuring responsible public officials.[38] On the other hand, the authors of *Federalist 53* understood keenly the benefits of long tenure:

> A few of the members [they wrote], as happens in all such assemblies, will possess superior talents; will, by frequent reelections, become members of long standing; will be thoroughly masters of the public business, and perhaps not unwilling to avail themselves of those advantages.[39]

Among the most significant developments in the Congressional system is surely the rise of long-tenured members who are "not unwilling to avail themselves of those advantages" conferred by long service.

Another feature of the Congressional career is what T. Richard Witmer has called "the aging of the House."[40] Contemporary members of the House are somewhat older than members were in earlier periods in our history (see Figure 2–E). Although short-term shifts often occur, the average age of Congressmen has been relatively steadily on the rise since the middle of the nineteenth century. In 1847, members of the 30th Congress averaged 42 years of age; in the 70th Congress, eighty years later, the average had risen to 53 years. Subsequently the average age has turned downward, though only slightly.

These factors—lengthening tenure and rising age of members—are influenced only in part by the age at which members are first elected to Congress. As indicated in Figure 2–E, the age of freshman Congressmen has varied somewhat erratically, changing roughly with the average age of all members. In the past two generations the age of incoming Congressmen has dropped significantly, a development probably responsible for the slight decline in average age of the entire membership. The same period, of course, has witnessed a rise in the average tenure of members. Witmer believes the decline in age of first-termers has had no effect on the lengthening of tenure itself, and there seems no reason to doubt that judgment.[41]

One possible explanation for rising Congressional tenure is the increase in life expectancy. Since the turn of the century, life

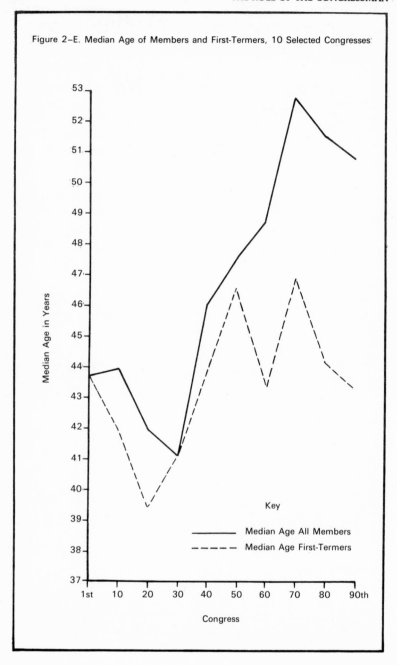

Figure 2–E. Median Age of Members and First-Termers, 10 Selected Congresses

expectancy for a 40-year-old man has risen by approximately four years, or two Congressional terms; for a 60-year-old man, it has risen by two years, or a single term.[42] This factor alone could account for much of the increase in age and tenure of Congressmen. But it is probable that other, more political factors were also at work.

The underlying development has probably been increasing acceptance of House service as a career. Formerly, a Representative was apt to look upon House service as a rung on a ladder to other political offices; today he is likely to view the House as a career in its own right. Evidence for this conclusion is found not only in decreased turnover and increased tenure, but also in decline in public office holding *after* the Congressional career. In the early nineteenth century, Young discovered, an average of 5.8 per cent of the members resigned during each Congress. This figure is about twice that for recent Congresses. And of those who resigned during the period Young examined, more than two thirds later held public offices outside Washington. "It was not," he concludes, "from the political vocation that the members tended to resign, but rather from the Washington community."[43] "While there were a few for whom the Hill was more than a way station in the pursuit of a career," he further observes, "a man's affiliation with the congressional community tended to be brief."[44] The Congress of the early nineteenth century clearly was incapable of sustaining the loyalty needed to induce its members to continue in office.

The contemporary Congress could hardly be a greater contrast. The separation of party and committee leadership hierarchies —an accomplishment of the Progressive revolt against Speaker Joseph G. Cannon early in the present century—broadened the number of leadership posts open to members on the basis of long service.[45] This development was not reversed when the Legislative Reorganization Act of 1946 decreased the number of standing committees. The act may have strengthened the seniority system itself, because with fewer committees longer tenure was generally required for a member to reach the top of his committee. Nor are party posts bestowed on the young. Leadership responsibility often came early to nineteenth-century Congressmen: Henry Clay, perhaps the most conspicuous example, was elected Speaker of the House while a freshman. Such an occurrence would be unthinkable today. John McCormack (D-Mass.) waited 35 years before gaining the Speakership in 1961; Sam Rayburn (D-Tex.), his predecessor, served 27 years before attaining that office. No Speaker in this century has been elected with fewer than 15 years' service in the House.[46] Apprenticeship for other leadership positions has also become extensive.

Proliferation of careers within the House has been accompanied by isolation of Congressional service from other elite careers. Huntington only slightly exaggerates the situation in observing that "leadership in the House of Representatives leads nowhere except to leadership in the House of Representatives."[47] During the nineteenth century Congressmen often left their posts after brief periods for other positions, many of which would today be thought far less prestigious than membership in the national legislature. Contemporary Congressmen, and especially Congressional leaders, are apt to retire or die in office—as in other professions. Even prestigious offices attract few Congressmen. Table 2-4, for example, reveals a decline in the proportion of Cabinet members with prior service in the House of Representatives. During the early nineteenth century many Cabinet members were recruited directly from Congress, sometimes in reward for supporting a successful Presidential candidate. Nowadays this practice is rare. The impression exists that lateral mobility from Congress to other positions has also dwindled. An obvious exception is mobility from House to Senate. Indeed, House membership is the most important prior office among present-day Senators, figuring in the careers of about one quarter of them.[48]

Table 2–4. Proportion of Cabinet Appointees with Congressional Experience, Selected Periods

Time Period	Per cent with Congressional Experience
1795–1832	67%
1861–1896	37
1897–1940	19
1941–1963	15

Source: Data from the period 1795–1832 are from Young, *The Washington Community*, p. 176. Other data are drawn from Huntington, *op. cit.*, p. 12.

What factors are associated with the rise of what we have called the Congressional career? That is, what permits and encourages long tenure of members? Careerism in elective office would certainly be impossible without conditions that encourage re-election of incumbents. Studies show that incumbents do enjoy overwhelming advantage at the polls over nonincumbent challengers.[49] Lacking adequate historical data on elections, we cannot pinpoint long-range trends with certainty; but there is reason to believe that the advantage of incumbency has grown and will continue to grow in the future.[50] One reason is that resources of men in office, in terms of staff, information, and access to media exposure, are likely to widen the "visibility gap" that separates incumbents from their opponents.

Another factor conducive to incumbency is low party competition. Congressional districts, because of their limited size, are more often one-party areas than are the larger statewide jurisdictions or the national electorate.[51] This tendency is fostered also by politicians who cunningly draw district lines so as to minimize political competition. Whatever the causes, the office of U.S. Representative is probably the least competitive office in our political system, above the local or county level. In only 23.4 per cent of the Congressional elections from 1914 to 1958 did a change in personnel take place; and in only 11.5 per cent was there a change in party control.[52] No doubt numerous other factors affect the electorate's disposition to re-elect incumbents: A favorable image of Congressional achievement or a period of economic prosperity, for instance, may enhance incumbents' chances for re-election.[53]* Such factors are complicated, and any comprehensive discussion would lead far afield of the present inquiry. What is essential is that political conditions have made long tenure possible.

Though re-election is a necessary condition, it is not sufficient for long tenure. Whatever the chances of re-election, incumbents must be motivated to try for office again. If the rewards of office are lacking—in terms of financial remuneration, or power, or prestige, or whatever—incumbents will have scant incentive to make a career of Congressional service. Other jobs will be more attractive, and legislators will lose little time in transferring to them if they can. This appears to have been the course of early legislators who found little reward in serving in the national legisla-

---

*As for economic conditions, Stuart A. Rice found a positive correlation between average tenure of Congressmen and business cycles in the period 1889–1923, "suggesting some degree of relationship between business prosperity and the state of mind in the electorate which results in the re-election of experienced Congressional incumbents."[54]

ture. Many resigned their posts, sometimes to take local offices.

In contrast, few of today's members would leave Congress for such reasons, and few at all leave Congress voluntarily. Several factors must have contributed to this development. The physical environment of the nation's capital may be one attraction (a statement no one could have made a century ago). The excitement and glamor of national politics, also, have increased compared to local politics. Thus, it is often said of modern Congressmen (and rarely said of their early predecessors) that "they never go back to Pocatello." (Even when retired involuntarily in an election, many contrive to remain in Washington, "where the action is.") Finally, the institution of Congress has probably risen in prestige, rendering it more satisfying to its members. Unfortunately, no data exist to put this proposition in historical perspective; but there is every evidence that the contemporary Congress, whatever its faults, remains a tantalizing goal for qualified political aspirants.[55] This is a crucial test of the health of an institution. Its ability to attract capable and ambitious men and women, and its capacity to hold them for long tenure through internal promotion indicate, much about an institution's success. On these grounds, at least, there is room for some satisfaction concerning the record of Congress.

A final aspect of the Congressional career—its demands upon incumbents—has little to do with recruitment. It has, however, a great deal to do with the impact of the institution on its members. The workload of the average Representative (or Senator) has risen impressively, by almost any measure one chooses to use.* This development has at least two types of career implications. First, the job is now full time for most members. It is extremely difficult (though not yet impossible) for a reasonably conscientious legislator to pursue another major occupation while serving in Congress. Secondly, the heavier workload is reflected in increasing interaction among members. This interaction leads in turn to the greater likelihood of shared roles and norms of behavior.

One measure of increasing interaction among members is the length of Congressional sessions, as set forth in Figure 2-F. These figures show that the average Congress (that is, all sessions be-

---

*Some components of the Congressional workload are described in Chapter 3.

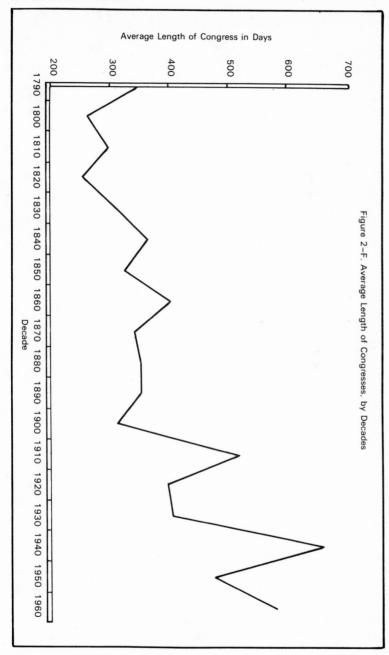

Figure 2-F. Average Length of Congresses, by Decades

tween one election and the next) is almost twice as long today as in 1900. Some of the rise is associated with wartime conditions, but even in peacetime the broadened governmental mandate has led to longer sessions. Of the thirteen Congressional sessions that have stretched over an entire year, for example, all but one have occurred in this century and all but two since 1940. The 1960's seem to have marked the advent of the year-round session as a common fact of Capitol Hill life: The average session was longer than in any other decade except the 1940's. Longer sessions were accompanied by longer working days, more bills, more new statutes, more constituent requests, and broader scope of activity —trends that are not likely to be reversed.

The fact that face-to-face interaction among members is more pervasive than ever before has important consequences for the operation of Congress as a system. The roles taken by actors in such a system (that is, norms or expectations of behavior) should be generally harmonious—more so at least than in a group characterized by only casual or sporadic interaction. We would further anticipate that institutional loyalty would be relatively high, other factors being equal. Finally, group-centered roles should have relatively great strength compared to roles centered on external objects, perhaps even including the member's constituency. These hypotheses are another way of saying that a full-time institution is more salient to its members than casual or sporadic association. No historical data exist on role-taking, of course, but we would expect the roles found among Congressmen in the late twentieth century to exhibit clearly the characteristics listed above—far more so than roles assumed by Congressmen in the days when Congressional life was confined to an unpleasant few months in Washington away from one's family and occupation.

CONCLUSIONS: CAREERS AND ROLES

In describing the status of members of Congress, we have explored such factors as occupations, political backgrounds, and geographic mobility; in describing the Congressional career, we have examined age, tenure, and certain aspects of the shared Washington experience. These attributes, taken by themselves, are useful in describing the characteristics of Congressmen as decision-makers and members of a political elite. At the most general level, several findings have been discussed in this chapter. First, members are recruited almost wholly from the same relatively high-status occupations. Although there does not seem to be a narrowing or rigidifying of the occupational base over a period of time, the limited number of occupations represented, as well as their specialized training and skills, would seem to have important implications for members' role perceptions. Second, the members are, and apparently have always been, political professionals who have served long and varied apprenticeship prior to election. Third, most Congressmen display long and intimate association with the geographic localities that elect them. Their geographic base of experience is probably not narrower than that of the general public, but it is limited in comparison to more cosmopolitan life histories found among other relevant elite groups. Finally, the job of Representative has definitely become a distinctive career, even to the extent of being autonomous from other political careers.

Characteristics like these indicate several things about the political system of which these legislators are a part. First, they tell us who is "entitled" to hold public office in our political system. On numerous counts, the office of U.S. Representative is subject to extremely selective recruitment—far more selective than the legal requirements. What effects this fact has upon the aspirations or behaviors of those so included or excluded, one can only speculate. Whatever the case, the selectivity itself does not necessarily imply that those who are excluded or under-represented are denied a meaningful political voice, in either a real or a psychological sense.

The backgrounds and career attributes of members also have relevance to the roles members assume in performing their legislative tasks. Such attributes, of course, do not by themselves create the roles assumed by the legislators. We have already cautioned against hasty inferences concerning the content of legislative roles based on the fact, for example, that many members are lawyers or that they have experienced little geographic mobility. In the chapters to follow, these background factors will be examined as they relate to role-perceptions. For certain types of roles, these variables have some explanatory power; for many others, however, other variables prove far more useful. Therefore, we will also examine what may be called "political variables"—

namely, the nature of the member's constituency and his particular position within the House of Representatives.

An underlying theme of this chapter has been that whatever the impact on the *content* of roles articulated by members, these background variables affect the over-all *dimensions* and *characteristics* of the role patterns. Specifically, we would hypothesize the following about the roles assumed by a group of the characters we have described: First, the relative homogeneity of the collectivity suggests that the range of articulated roles will be moderate rather than extreme. And if prior occupation is of consequence, roles ought to stress the twin norms of advocacy or entrepreneurship, and of negotiation or compromise. However, the conflicting demands of the member's geographic base of operation and his Congressional career may produce cross-pressures that would be reflected in tension between constituency-centered and task- or group-centered roles. We would further expect group-based roles to be increasingly widely shared and salient, given the increasing continuities of the Congressional career. Finally, all of the roles should be highly verbalized and precisely articulated, given the high social and professional status of members.

Some of these attributes will emerge from the findings presented in subsequent chapters. Other attributes, while they may appear to be present, cannot be verified because of the lack of comparative data—from other time periods or from other political elite groups. To the extent that these role characteristics are borne out, they would reflect an institution fundamentally cohesive but embodying deep potentiality for dissension. An institution with well articulated, widely shared norms should, other things being equal, provide a satisfying environment for its members. This satisfying environment, it should be stressed, is a product not only of compatible backgrounds but also of complementary role-perceptions made possible by those backgrounds. Moreover, the stress upon fiduciary advocacy and bargaining is compatible with the function of the legislator in our society—even though these twin role-imperatives may yield very real tensions for members in the vicissitudes of decision-making.

Notwithstanding the probable viability of an institution composed of the kinds of members we have described, at least one important source of role conflict is indicated. The member's career, not to mention his electoral fate, is essentially constituency-oriented. Yet the task situation facing him on Capitol Hill, and the group environment that increasingly surrounds him, requires that his outlook also be task- or group-centered. Thus, the member may experience a very deep tension between the requirements of his constituency and those of his job. This tension is not merely, or even necessarily, a product of the stresses and strains of bargaining; it is rather a conflict of roles internalized by the member himself. This is not a new or unique problem: It has been expressed in one way or another by legislators at least since the time of Edmund Burke. But it assumes special relevance in the context of the present inquiry, and in reference to the contemporary American Congress. Compatability and conflict among roles will be discussed as we turn to the general question of how the legislator perceives and describes his job.

CHAPTER 3

THE JOB OF
THE CONGRESSMAN

Thus far our inquiry has sought to accomplish two objectives. The first has been to view members of Congress as participants in a distinctive system of behaviors—a system emphasizing bargaining and negotiation, and called "legislative." The second objective has been to examine several formal attributes of members of the U.S. House of Representatives, in order to describe Representatives as a group of political decision-makers and to suggest several hypotheses concerning the probable nature of their role definitions. In other words, we have attempted to generate propositions about the roles of Congressmen by using conceptual premises and career data.

The actual roles that Congressmen assume in performing their tasks (or rather, evidence concerning those roles) form the subject of the remainder of the book. The primary unit of analysis is the *role cognition*—how members of Congress conceive and express their norms of behavior. Of course, several techniques are available for gathering information on the roles of political actors. Some are limited to describing the institutional framework in which the decision-makers operate; others entail conceptual analysis of the type presented in Chapter 1; still others necessitate detailed audits of the social attributes, as in Chapter 2. Sooner or later, however, the student must penetrate the decision-makers' own environment to ferret out empirical evidence of the role or roles they assume in their daily work. Elaborate tests of the legislators' performances may be devised—analyzing, for example, floor or committee deliberations or voting choices. Or, as in this study, the student may choose to elicit responses from the legislators themselves by means of a survey protocol. Whatever method is chosen, the evidence must emanate from the legislators themselves.

THE ROLE CONCEPT

The concept of role is crucial to the study of social systems. "For most purposes," Parsons explains, *"the conceptual unit of the social system is the role.* It is the point of contact between the system of action of the individual actor and the social system."[1] Although used somewhat differently by anthropologists, psychologists, and sociologists, the term helps to define an actor's functional position in a system of action. As Thibault and Kelley explain,

> Roles consist of clusters of norms providing for a division of labor or specialization of functions among the members of a group. A person is said to occupy a particular role when, in relation to some special social or task area, the norms applicable to his behavior are different from those applicable to [others].[2]

Thus, a role is an expected pattern of behaviors associated with an actor who is in a particular relationship to a social system. The role constitutes, in turn, a behavioral method of defining his place, or status, within that system. "A role represents the dynamic aspect of a status."[3] Or as Gabriel Almond expresses the relationship, a role is "that organized sector of an actor's orientation which constitutes and defines his participation in an interactive process."[4]

The occupant of any given social position plays a number of roles as he responds to his environment. The legislator, of course, lives and works in a complex environment; and he therefore assumes a number of roles. He is not distinguished by performing a legislative role, but rather a *set of roles* through which he relates to his tasks and to relevant "others" in his environment.[5] A diagram that suggests the multiple roles of legislators is found in Figure 3–A.[6] A key segment of role behavior is what Wahlke and his colleagues call the *core-roles sector,* which includes "all norms guiding the legislator's behavior with reference to other legislators perceived simply in their character (or role) as one of all coequal legislators, or with reference to the legislature perceived as a type of social situation or a sort of 'generalized other'."[7] This sector

embraces several role dimensions that together define in the broadest terms what it means to be a legislator. These include the
purposive role, which embodies norms concerning "the substantive
goals or purposes of legislation and the legislative operation";[8]
the representational roles, or *style and focus of representation,* adopted
by the member; and the consensual role (or roles), "those unwrit-
ten but informally understood norms sometimes called rules-of-
the-game."[9] The present study permits no exploration of the last-
mentioned category; but purposive and representational roles will
be examined in this and the following chapter.

In addition, the legislator assumes numerous roles in interacting
with important "others" who, whether inside or outside the legislature, impinge directly upon the legislative system of behavior.
These actors (who usually represent other systems of behavior)
include constituents, political party leaders, interest-group spokesmen, and the President and other members of the executive
branch. Also relevant upon occasion are family, kinship, or asso-
ciational groups. Finally, the legislator may perform specialized
roles by virtue of his rank or position within the legislature—for
example, party leader, committee chairman, committee member,
or expert on some substantive issue or problem. The legislator is,
then, a composite of the roles he plays as he interacts with others
to perform his tasks.

Not only does a single actor play many roles in such a complex
interactive process as legislation, but the roles themselves can be
defined and measured by the observer in several ways. Roles may
be derived, for example, by analyzing the actor's behavior patterns (enacted roles), by reference to other people's ideas about
what he *will* do (expectations), by reference to other people's
ideas about what he *should* do (norms), or by probing his own
expressed standards of behavior (role cognitions).[10] Nor are these
aspects of role unrelated: In any social situation an actor responds
to expectations and norms that others associate with incumbents
of his position, as well as to his own assessment of his position.

Given the numerous roles that any Congressman plays, he may
quite possibly experience conflict among them. Nor is there any
assurance that he will define his roles in the same way that his
colleagues do. And to complicate matters further, the expectations
others hold for his behavior may diverge from his own conceptions. Thus, conflict as well as consensus on roles is inevitable.[11]

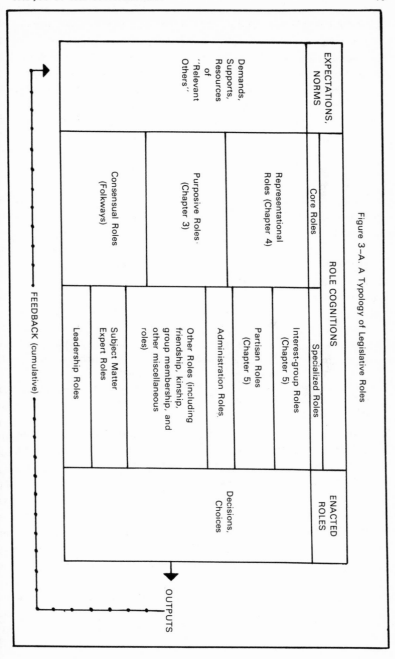

Figure 3–A. A Typology of Legislative Roles

This conflict may occur within a single role, as when two lobby-ists urge the Representative to vote on opposite sides of the same question. Or it may occur between two or more roles, as when the member is torn (as he may often be) between his role as party loyalist and his role as defender of his constituency's interests. As for the role expectations that outsiders hold for Congressmen, this matter must await further research.[12] An important problem, on which our analysis may cast some light, is the extent to which the roles of Congressmen are complementary or conflicting.

Role analysis offers several distinct advantages for the student of legislative behavior. First, and not the least important, because the concept has been utilized by other investigators, it permits comparisons among several specific subgroups of the *genus* legis-lator. Second, the role concept yields a relatively comprehensive picture of the legislator and his responses to multiple aspects of his environment. Third, it treats empirical and behavioral evidence in the framework of concepts which have proved themselves in a variety of analytic contexts. And finally, in the words of Wahlke and his associates, the notion of role

yields a model of the legislator as an acting human individual which is consistent with the basic understandings of individual and group psychology. At the same time, it yields a model of the legislature as an institutionalized human group which logically incorporates the model of the individual legislator and which re-lates the behavior of legislators to problems of legislative structure and function which are the traditional concern of students in the field.[13]

In other words, the concept of role represents a linkage of the behavioral study of legislators with the institutional concerns so familiar to our everyday understandings of political life.

Our data concerning role cognitions were derived from a series of open-ended questions administered to a sample of members of the U.S. House of Representatives. The attitudes expressed, while obtained in the somewhat rarified atmosphere of the inter-view situation, are in theory relatively close to the actual choices that Congressmen must make in the performance of their daily tasks. The over-all assumption is that

a significant proportion of legislators' behavior is role behavior, that this behavior is substantially congruent with their role con-cepts, and that insight into the working of legislative bodies can therefore be gained by ascertaining their role concepts.[14]

For this reason, the responses may be considered a form of behavior that can be related to independent demographic or political variables. As evidence of predispositions to act in certain ways, moreover, the responses may be treated as independent variables with regard to actual patterns of choices revealed in, for instance, voting behavior.

METHODOLOGY OF THE STUDY

The data on which this study is based were gathered through a sample survey of members of the House of Representatives during the 88th Congress (1963-1964). For the survey three samples were employed. The first of these, a random, or general, sample, consisted of eighty-seven completed interviews stratified by party and leadership position. Thus, the completed sample possessed the same ratio of Democrats to Republicans as the House as a whole; and within each party grouping, the proportion of leaders to nonleaders was the same as that actually existing in the House.* Respondents in each of these four groupings (Democratic and Republican leaders and nonleaders) were selected on a random basis from a list of all members of the House.

In the present study, the random sample of eighty-seven members will be drawn upon unless otherwise indicated. However, two additional groups of Congressmen were surveyed. A randomly drawn leadership over-sample of twenty-three members holding formal leadership positions permitted analysis of differences in attitudes between leaders and nonleaders. Interviews were also completed with the six Representatives from the "top leadership" of both parties who had not been selected in either of the random sampling procedures.† Because of the limited size of the samples, the findings should be interpreted as suggestive rather than conclusive in indicating factors associated with role-taking in the House. A detailed discussion of the methods employed in the survey is found in the Appendix.

*Those classified as leaders held one or more of the following positions in the 88th Congress: committee chairmen and ranking minority members; chairmen and ranking minority members of Appropriations subcommittees; Speaker, Majority Leader, and Majority Whip; and Minority Leader, Minority Whip, and Republican Conference Chairman.

†The universe of top formal leaders included the chairmen and ranking minority members of the Appropriations, Rules, and Ways and Means committees, as well as the Speaker, Majority Leader, and Majority Whip, and the Minority Leader, Minority Whip, and Republican Conference Chairman.

In probing the members' role cognitions, key portions of the interview protocol drew upon the 1962 study of four state legislatures by Wahlke and his associates.[15] Specifically, a series of questions was designed to elicit the members' perceptions of their roles. These items were, in order:

(1) First of all, how would you describe the job of being a Congressman—what are the most important things you should do here?

(2) Now, what are the most pressing problems you face in trying to do your job as Congressman—what are the things that hinder you in your tasks?

(3) Now let's turn briefly to the role of Congress as a *whole* and its place in our government. . . . First, what role should Congress play in our governmental system—what should its functions be?

(4) How effective is Congress (and especially the House) in fulfilling the role(s) you feel it should play?

(5) What are the most pressing problems which prevent Congress from doing what you think it ought to do?*

These items were broad enough to elicit a number of attitude dimensions, only some of which were applicable to the concept of role. Although the initial question was the one used most frequently by other students, the remaining items also triggered role-relevant responses in many instances. Coders therefore were instructed to inspect responses to all of these items before recording codes on the role dimensions relevant to this inquiry. With only minor modifications and refinements, the codes proposed by Wahlke and his associates provided a surprisingly close fit with the Congressmen's responses.[16]

PURPOSIVE ROLES

What priorities do legislators hold in their total conception of their tasks and responsibilities? Unfortunately, this question is difficult to resolve with any degree of certainty. Given the complex

---

*The complete survey instrument is reproduced in the Appendix.

structure of roles assumed by each member of Congress, virtually
a total map of role subsets for every member would be needed to
assess the over-all priority of various roles; and even then, assign-
ing relative weights to the numerous role subsets would be
hazardous.

Role analysis, however, provides one means of estimating the
over-all weight that Congressmen assign to various legislative
functions. This is the concept of the purposive, or substantive,
role. The purposive role dimension is unquestionably the most
inclusive of those uncovered by various students. It is the legislator's conception of the ultimate aim of his activities, of "the
where-from and what-for of legislative action."[17] As Wahlke and
his associates concluded, the purposive role dimension is "shaped
by both historic conceptions of the functions of the legislature
and by contemporary circumstances in the governmental power
structure."[18] The distribution of role orientations along this
dimension should thus provide a rough indication of the importance of various activities in the Congressman's scheme of things.

The distribution of purposive roles is shown in Table 3-1. For
each of the eighty-seven Congressional respondents, a dominant,
or "primary," role could be discerned from analysis of the completed interviews, although most respondents also evidenced from
one to three subsidiary role orientations. (The eighty-seven Congressmen indicated an average of 2.1 role orientations; and only
22 per cent possessed but a single role orientation.) Interestingly,
the average Congressman expressed a slightly greater number of
purposive roles than legislators in three of the four states examined
by Wahlke and his associates.[19]* This variation in response pattern may be traceable to differences in the sophistication of the
respondents, or to differences in the complexity of the political
environment, or to some other factor.

The role of the Tribune is clearly strongest in the minds of the
Congressmen, as Table 3-1 indicates. This role orientation could
be taken as the classic definition of the legislator-as-representative
in a democratic polity: the discoverer, reflector, or advocate of
popular needs and wants. As a senior Republican expressed it,

> Represent the people . . . that's the first duty . . . do exactly
> what the name "Representative" implies. [Midwestern Republican
> leader, rural district]

*The exception was New Jersey.

**Table 3-1. Distribution of Purposive Roles
Among 87 Members of the House of Representatives**

Purposive Role	Members Listing Role as Primary	Members Listing Role as Secondary	Total Members Listing Role[a]	Role as Per cent of All Roles Mentioned
Tribune	47%	33%	82%	40%
Ritualist	41	24	67	33
Inventor	7	23	31	15
Broker	4	13	17	8
Opportunist	1	7	8	4
Total	100%	100%		100%
(n)	(87)	(91)		(178)

a Since many members articulated more than one role, the sum of the per cent of members indicating all of the roles considerably exceeds 100 per cent.

The Tribune role is historically rooted in the legislator's function of fighting the people's battles against the Crown, a fact which led such theorists as John Locke to give the legislator a paramount place in the polity. On this side of the Atlantic, the colonial legislator was often expected to defend the interests of his neighbors and constituents against the interests of the Crown and its appointed governors. Today, some form of the representative role is the quality most frequently ascribed to Congressmen by the public.[20] Thus, the dominance of the Tribune role is consistent both with historical conceptions of the legislative task and current public expectations of performance.

The Tribune, like other purposive role orientations, is an extremely inclusive category. A Republican first-termer, ruminating on his tasks, gave the following characterization:

> Taking care of home problems. Case work, not necessarily having anything to do with legislation at all. Taking care of constituents. In the legislative part of it, getting legislation through that affects your district. [Western Republican nonleader, rural district]

Moreover, the Tribune role may be held in conjunction with other purposive roles. In the following comment, for example, the Congressman combines a basic concern for representation (Tribune) with the need for mastery of legislative procedures (Ritualist):

> My job is primarily one of communications. This is a two-way situation. It is important to understand your constituents, so that you can adequately transmit their feelings and ideas to the people

in Washington. At the same time, you must be able to convey these ideas successfully on the floor or in committee. [Midwestern Republican nonleader, mixed district]

Tribunes may define their constituencies in various ways—a point to be considered in greater detail later. Consider, however, this not atypical expression by a Congressional Tribune:

Primarily [my job is] to represent the thinking and philosophy of the people at home; but the country at large is also important. "What is good for America." Fortunately, the two coincide in most cases. . . . In practical terms, there is the political fact that textiles are important in my area. . . . But because of ties with the textile industry [nationally] its implications carry on to national issues. [Southern rural nonleader, Democrat]

It is important to note, therefore, that it matters not to *which* constituents the member's ear is attuned, nor even *how* he comes to ascertain their interests. The only requirement is that the Tribune perceive himself as a spokesman for the people.

The frequency of the Tribune role was not altogether anticipated. In fact, Wahlke and his associates produced slightly different findings: In all of the states (California, Ohio, New Jersey, and Tennessee) the Ritualist role was most frequently articulated. The Tribune role was second in frequency in three of the states; in Ohio it ranked third. Conceivably the variance in findings is an artifact of difference in the coding process; but this seems unlikely in view of the clarity with which the roles were described in the earlier study, and the ease with which the Congressional responses fitted into the described categories.

A more persuasive reason for the variance would be some fundamental difference between the two types of legislative bodies. It seems reasonable to argue that in comparison with state legislators, Representatives perceive themselves more visible to their constituents and devote more time to dealing with constituency problems. Representatives no doubt sense that communications media have made their voters more aware of certain national issues and more apt to turn to them for help in resolving problems. Thus, a Congressional office (if not the Representative himself) devotes large amounts of time to constituent mail and "casework." State legislators, in contrast, undoubtedly receive less mail, have less office contact, and typically have no staff help in dealing with district affairs. These are speculations and do not, of

course, provide a definitive explanation for the slight discrepancy
in findings. All that can be said at this point is that, assuming
the data in both cases to be valid, members of the House of Representatives appear to place somewhat more emphasis upon their
tasks as representatives than do members of the state legislatures
studied.

The second predominant role orientation, that of the Ritualist,
in contrast turns the member's sights inward to the institution.
It must be remembered that Congress itself imposes many limitations on the behavior of its members, for it is an ongoing institution that has evolved a veritable maze of rules, procedures,
duties, privileges, etiquettes, and informal understandings. To be
effective, newly minted members must learn their way around this
maze; and many more experienced members devote much of their
energy to cultivating these traditions. The Ritualist thus emphasizes the formal aspects of Capitol Hill duties and routines—
legislative work, investigation and overseeing, and committee
specialization.

Despite its label, the Ritualist role need not be (and usually
is not) narrow or technical in scope: It includes a very broad
range of the member's activities as seen and assessed by his
Capitol Hill colleagues, and it conforms with frequently expressed
norms of legislative behavior.[21] Consider, for example, the following comments of Ritualists in our survey:

> Write the laws. Control the purse-strings. . . . Do your home-
> work. . . . [Midwestern rural leader, Republican]

> I tend to legislative matters—committee work, where the spade-
> work is done; and I remain on deck when fighting is in progress
> on legislation—to be present and deliberate. For me, work on the
> floor and in committee is most important. This is where the work
> is done. [Southern Republican leader, urban-rural district]

> To vote in committee or on the floor, to understand the legis-
> lation, to gain a reputation within your committee to the point
> that other members respect your vote and take your advice.
> Effectiveness in your committee is the most important part of
> your job. . . . [Midwestern urban nonleader, Democrat]

The Ritualist role is therefore closely associated with the House
norm that a member should specialize in a substantive policy
area—normally in his committee assignment—and then "do his
homework":

All of us have to become specialists along certain lines. [Southern Democratic leader, rural district]

Successful performance of this role yields influence, inasmuch as colleagues will be inclined to invest their trust in the member's knowledge and expertise. Because time is short and decisions numerous, Ritualists are often relied upon to supply information on the substance and status of legislation. As one of many respondents expressed it,

Well, it's a hectic life. Once you have seniority, there's more pressure. Often there's little time to consider how to vote; you must rely on people who can be trusted who are on the appropriate committee. . . . [Southern rural nonleader, Democrat]

The effective House careerist, then, is "a worker, a specialist, and a craftsman—someone who will concentrate his energies in a particular field and gain prestige and influence in that."[22]

Nor is the Ritualist unconcerned about his representative tasks. Often the member's legislative expertise arises from his concern for issues of interest to his constituents. Former Congressman Frank E. Smith (D-Miss.) relates how his interest in flood control and water resource development, policies of direct concern to his district, led him to seek membership on the Public Works Committee. "The interests of my district dictated my field of specialization," he explains, ". . . but the decision to specialize in some legislative field is automatic for the member who wants to exercise any influence."[23] Similar testimony could be given by many, perhaps most, members of Congress.

Another type of Ritualist is the party leader. For him the chores of party organization, procedural manipulation, or "counting the House" (to give a few examples) arise from his formal position as well as his personal interests. One Ritualist, a top Democratic leader, spoke of his role as follows:

Ever since I came to Congress, I have been greatly concerned with my membership in the party as a working organization. I had what I believe was a fairly mature belief in the progressive policies of the Democratic party, along with an understanding that one individual cannot immediately have a terrific impact.

[In my present position] my most important job is to insure that major policies are created through joint Executive-Congressional discussion which allows the leadership to go along with concessions. In these negotiations, I play a substantive and procedural role. . . . [Southern rural leader, Democratic]

Obviously, not many members devote such undivided attention to this aspect of the Ritualist role; but for this man, and for a few of his colleagues, it is virtually a full-time preoccupation.

The Tribune and Ritualist roles pervaded our interviews to such a degree that it seems reasonable to think of them as representing a consensus of what the Representative's job is all about. No less than eighty-two per cent of the respondents expressed some form of the Tribune conception; fully two thirds gave evidence of the Ritualist role. Taken together, these roles describe the way in which most incumbents view the substance of *the* legislative task. Recent scholarly literature has tended to stress cues that originate and circulate internally within the legislature; and the relative frequency of the Ritualist role suggests that this emphasis is not without foundation. Yet, at the same time, the incidence of the Tribune role suggests that representational functions (however they may be conceived by the member) continue to hold an important place in the minds of contemporary Congressmen. Taken together, these two role orientations express the general responses of members to the two most important components of their environment: their external publics, and their colleagues on the Hill.

Although these two roles were the dominant purposive orientations among our sample of Congressmen, the three additional roles found by Wahlke and his associates appeared in the interviews with sufficient frequency and distinctiveness to be considered as separate types. Next in frequency is the Inventor role, one which emphasizes problem-solving or policy innovation—"getting (certain) things done." As one Congressional Inventor expressed his functions,

> The first demand on us is the legislative program, in its national and international aspects. One must, of course, be a legislator. . . . Then, there are the things you crusade for—for example, a Humane Society bill, renewal of servicemen's life insurance [and so forth]. . . . [Midwestern suburban-rural nonleader, Democrat]

Though Inventors are most frequently found in the liberal camp, consider the following comments of conservative Inventors in our sample:

> We can be likened to the directors of a going business organization: we must see that it operates well, and that it operates in the *black*. We are custodians of other people's money, and that's one of the most responsible duties. . . . [Southern urban nonleader, Republican]

Now, a member of Congress must be a state, and United States, and even a world representative, because the world revolves around the United States and around Congress. Even businessmen want us to help them run their businesses. . . .

On the shoulders of [my] committee rests largely the future of the United States. We must protect the stability of the dollar. History shows that reckless spending leads to bankruptcy. We have to stop this tendency. [Criticizes British Fabian socialism at length.] The majority in Congress have no regard for *our* concept of government—that is, they spend and spend—which will destroy the country. . . .

What we *must* do is put the government on a double-entry bookkeeping system, "debit" on one side of the ledger, "credit" on the other. The systems they use now are terrible: It's impossible to understand—too complicated. Why, you can't even get a statement from an agency on how much money has been spent! We must go back to debit and credit, just like when I kept books at the _____ Lumber Company. [Midwestern rural leader, Republican]

Some members focus the Inventor role around their committee work, as in the above comment. Others consider it a complement to the Tribune role, saying in effect that some issues require them to be constituency spokesmen while others demand creative thought on their part.

Next in frequency (about four per cent of the respondents considered it their primary role) is the classic role of brokerage—that is, the Congressman as politician in a pluralistic society, balancing and blending diverse geographic, occupational, or ideological interests. Consider these expressions from Congressional Brokers:

The public has a false impression of Congress, an idea that all we do is talk. . . . We should be more like jurors than like attorneys. . . . More judging than talking. [Eastern suburban leader, Republican]

Doing what is best for the country while representing to our best ability the views of the district. When these are in conflict, it is usually capable of being reconciled. . . . [Eastern rural nonleader, Republican]

To anticipate briefly the discussion of the following chapter, it must be pointed out that the Broker role, insofar as it refers to striking balances between the interests of the member's district and those of the nation at large, lies very close to the notion of a balanced-area focus.* The essence of the Broker role, however, is

*See Chap. 4, p. 124.

the fact that brokerage represents a substantive interest, not merely a means of evaluating or resolving competing constituency claims.

The small number of Brokers may seem surprising, especially in view of our earlier description of legislation as a bargaining process. There are even fewer Brokers in Congress than in the four legislatures studied by Wahlke and his associates, and no explanation for the disparity is readily available. However, the relative scarcity of Brokers—both in Congress and the state legislatures—may not be as inconsistent as it appears at first glance. After all, fiduciary bargainers seek to advance the particular interests of their clients, and it is only as all legislators play out this imperative that brokerage occurs. Hence, it is reasonable to suppose that brokerage is subsumed in such purposive orientations as Tribune and Ritualist, not to mention consensual norms, or folkways. The fact that fiduciary bargainers do not as a rule perceive brokerage as their major substantive concern is therefore not an incongruity.

The role of the Opportunist is very rare in the House. This role stresses the job of campaigning and gaining re-election.† As one former member expressed this orientation, "All members of Congress have a primary interest in being re-elected. Some members have no other interest."[26] Or, as it was put by the one respondent who indicated this was his primary role,

> Well, getting re-elected. I really can't do much better than that [in answering this question]. [Eastern suburban nonleader, Republican]

Several other respondents, while manifesting other role orientations, reminded the interviewer that, after all, re-election was a prerequisite to anything else they might be able to accomplish in the House. "You can't be a statesman unless you get elected" is a common saying on Capitol Hill. Two respondents expressed this concern as follows:

† Contrast this description with the one advanced in Wahlke *et al.*—That is, the Opportunist as one who plays *at* the legislative role but who is really playing other, extra-legislative roles.[24] It is interesting that Wahlke and his colleagues apparently found no evidence of the role as they defined it, for one would assume it would be held by at least a significant minority of state legislators. From depth interviews with freshman legislators in Connecticut, James David Barber found a number of respondents who might fit this role.[25] No evidence of such roles was found among the House respondents, but this is not surprising in view of the relatively greater physical and psychological demands which membership in Congress makes upon incumbents.

As [former Congressman] Walter Judd used to say, you must be re-elected before you can be a good Congressman. . . . I don't enjoy having to cater to the irrelevant aspects of this job in order to be re-elected. [Western urban nonleader, Republican]

Well, getting settled here in Washington has been my basic problem, but now I have to worry about getting re-elected. [Western suburban nonleader, Democrat]

While the Opportunist role was too rare in our sample to permit any meaningful statistical generalizations, it may be of interest that 72 per cent of all those expressing the role (whether primary or secondary) represented competitive Congressional districts (that is, those won by less than 60 per cent of the vote in the previous election). Given this fact, it is hardly surprising that these men should give re-election a high place among their tasks.

What types of Congressmen express each of the various purposive conceptions of the office? Put another way, what factors are associated with the role cognitions just described? Our data do not throw much light on this question, for reasons that must be apparent from the foregoing discussion of the relative frequency of the various purposive roles. The Tribune and Ritualist conceptions are the only ones expressed by sufficient members of Representatives to permit meaningful analysis of variables. Yet precisely because these roles represent so wide a consensus, they do not serve to differentiate legislators from one another. Nonetheless, several interesting differences appear if we consider only the respondents' primary purposive orientations. We shall point out a few of these findings in the following pages; but it must be emphasized that determination of the primary role for each respondent rested upon the judgment of the author and his co-researchers in their analysis of the completed interviews.

Broadly speaking, the range of possible independent variables may be divided into two groups: *nonpolitical* and *political*. Of the former group of variables, those not overtly political in nature, some are psychological and others are socioeconomic. The present research design did not permit exploration of psychological determinants—by standardized test items, much less by depth-interview techniques.* Several socioeconomic factors, including the so-called "social background" variables explored in the previous chapter,

---

*The difficulty of administering such interview schedules to members of elite groupings is an obvious deterrent to widespread use.[27]

were analyzed. Of the second group of variables—those more properly classed as political—some are external to Congress (*e.g.,* constituency characteristics) and some are internal (*e.g.,* the member's position in the House). The Plimsoll line separating the political and the nonpolitical is somewhat arbitrary, of course, because nonpolitical factors may become politicized (that is, made politically relevant) in a variety of ways. The profession of law, it has already been noted, is for most practitioners a fact of social or economic significance; but it may also serve an individual as a door to political advancement.

The Congressman's background seems to have little impact upon *which* purposive role he assumes. His occupational training, his geographic mobility (or the lack of it), his political experience, his socioeconomic status—none of these variables is related strongly to purposive role.† This does not mean, of course, that such variables are unimportant in determining other kinds of behaviors. Nor does it prove such factors uninfluential in determining role perceptions. As already observed, the kinds of variables discussed in Chapter 2 may well set important limits on the range and style of roles evidenced in the House, even if not on the specific roles chosen by each of the members.

In two instances, however, background factors do appear to be related to purposive roles. One of these exceptions relates to occupation. Most observers see significance in the fact that lawyers tend to dominate American legislatures. However, the legal profession and the political career converge in so many respects that it is difficult to say just what impact legal backgrounds should have upon legislators' orientations.[28] Will the lawyer's skill in advocacy on behalf of clients lead him to take the Tribune role? Will his experience in negotiation lead him to play the Broker? Or will his technical expertise in the law induce him to concentrate on the complexities of the legislative process, as in the Ritualist role? Each of these dispositions might well grow out of a legal career. Indeed, this is what is meant by the "professional convergence" of law and politics, as applied to legislators.

The present findings nevertheless indicate certain differences

† Standard biographical information for respondents was obtained from such sources as *Congressional Directory, Who's Who in America,* and *Biographical Directory of the American Congress.* A written questionnaire submitted to the member's office provided a check on this information, in addition to information not available in the published sources—*e.g.,* father's occupation, annual income.

between the primary purposive role orientations of lawyers and those of members from other occupational backgrounds. The figures are presented in Table 3-2, which gives the proportion from each occupational grouping expressing the two major roles, Tribune and Ritualist.

**Table 3–2. Occupation and Primary Purposive
Roles of 87 Members of Congress**

| Purposive | Occupation | | |
Role	Law	Business	Other
Tribune	43%	62%	39%
Ritualist	43	33	46
Other	14	5	15
Total	100%	100%	100%
(n)	(53)	(21)	(13)

Lawyers are somewhat more likely to be Ritualists, and somewhat less likely to be Tribunes, than are members with business backgrounds. When primary and secondary roles are added together, this difference disappears. The lawyers' relative disinclination toward the Tribune role as primary focus, however, is fairly clear; and the same phenomenon was found in each of the state legislatures examined by Wahlke and his colleagues.[29] The finding suggests at least that the lawyers' experience as advocates does not lead them to give disproportionate importance to the Tribune orientation.

As will be seen presently, this phenomenon can be traced in large measure to partisan and regional differences. Democrats, and particularly southerners, are inclined toward the Ritualist role, and southern Democrats in turn are drawn disproportionately from legal backgrounds. However, it is relevant to observe that some differences appear within the occupational classifications, between full-time lawyers and those who have pursued law along with another occupation. Differences also appear among businessmen. This phenomenon is reflected in Table 3-3.

**Table 3–3. Lawyers, Businessmen, and Primary
Purposive Roles of 87 Members of the House**

Purposive Role	Law Only	Law-Combination	Nonlaw	Business Only	Business-Combination	Nonbusiness
Tribune	38%	56%	53%	64%	50%	43%
Ritualist	43	44	43	27	50	43
Total (n)	(37)	(16)	(34)	(11)	(16)	(61)

As can be seen, full-time lawyers are much less apt to be Tribunes than lawyer colleagues who have also engaged in other
occupations. Indeed, the "lawyers-plus" more nearly resemble
nonlaw members than they do other lawyers. Among businessmen,
the opposite tendency is evident: Pure businessmen are strongly
inclined to favor the Tribune role over the Ritualist role, while
their "business-plus" counterparts more nearly resemble the non-
businessmen. This finding suggests (though it can do no more than
that) that members who have background in only a single profession are led to assume more distinctive primary role patterns
—Tribune for businessmen and non-Tribune roles for lawyers—
than are members who have practiced more than one occupation.

The member's political experience also impinges upon purposive
roles. First, those with extensive experience are more likely to
assume the Ritualist role than those with little experience. More
explicitly, former state legislators show much more affinity to the
Ritualist orientation than members who have not served in state
legislatures. These two findings, coupled with the earlier findings
concerning lawyers, lend the definite impression that in the House,
Ritualists are found disproportionately among political careerists.
The Ritualist role, more than the Tribune, seems to be the outgrowth of socialization that the politician receives through prior
political experience. This phenomenon will also be reflected as
purposive roles are compared with political variables.

A partisan breakdown of purposive roles is presented in Table
3–4. Democrats are clearly more prone to express the Ritualist role,

**Table 3–4. Party Affiliation and Primary Purposive
Roles Among 87 Members of the House**

Purposive Role	Democrats	Republicans
Tribune	40%	59%
Ritualist	45	35
Inventor	11	
Broker	4	3
Opportunist		3
Total	100%	100%
(n)	(53)	(34)

while Republicans are more often found in the ranks of the Tribunes. Perhaps the leadership status of the Democratic party is

responsible for the divergence. During the period of our study, Democrats controlled substantial majorities in both houses, not to mention the Presidency—a fact which gave them a responsibility for the legislative agenda, in which Republicans were only junior partners. (This would mean that the Ritualist role should be more prevalent among Republicans when they are the majority party—a proposition that obviously cannot be tested in the present study.) The parties also differ in other respects, and we will have an opportunity to examine these factors presently.

One further observation may be extracted from Table 3–4— though in this instance the number involved is small. First, the Inventors were exclusively Democrats. Although a few Republicans expressed the Inventor role as a secondary or subordinate theme (not recorded in the table), Democrats dominated the Inventor category. Inventors were, as mentioned earlier, decidedly more liberal ideologically than other purposive role groupings. Of those expressing primarily an Inventor focus, two thirds scored low (less than twenty per cent) on the *Congressional Quarterly's* "conservative coalition"[30] index for the 88th Congress—compared to one third or less within other purposive groupings.* (Indeed, Inventors were the only purposive group with distinctive ideological voting habits, as reflected by this measure.)

Length of tenure, or seniority, is perhaps the single most important determinant of the member's position within the House. Seniority itself may be considered a crude measure of the extent of the member's socialization to institutional norms, and it is linked to other key variables that affect his conception of his tasks. On the one hand, the type of district that elects the member is a determinant of seniority—in some cases virtually assuring long tenure, in others rendering it very difficult to achieve. On the other hand, seniority is the latchkey for most formal leadership positions in the House—including chairmanships and ranking minority posts of the standing committees and subcommittees. Formal leadership and seniority are thus closely intertwined. In an earlier account of the present research, it was argued that seniority—independent of formal leadership position—influences

---

*Coalition-support scores for each respondent were computed by dividing the percentage of times each supported the coalition in the 88th Congress by the sum of his coalition-support percentage and his coalition-opposition percentage. This procedure removed the effect of absences during roll-call votes.

members' attitudes toward structural and procedural reform of Congress.[31] Its association with purposive roles, however, is less impressive.

Table 3–5. Seniority and Primary Purposive Roles of 87 Members of the House

Purposive Role	Members, By Seniority		
	One Term	2–5 Terms	6–plus Terms
Tribune	53%	42%	50%
Ritualist	23	47	44
Inventor	12	6	6
Broker	6	6	
Opportunist	6		
Total	100%	101%	100%
(n)	(17)	(36)	(34)

The most striking aspect of Table 3–5—the increasing numbers of Ritualists after the freshman year in Congress—is an anticipated phenomenon: As the new member is socialized into House work and routine, he becomes ever more immersed in the substantive content of its business. Quickly he is advised to develop a policy specialization (usually in an area within his committee's jurisdiction) and to become known as one who "does his homework." One of our interviewees, an acknowledged expert in his policy field, described his experiences as follows:

> Attending committee meetings is my most important job. It's the only way to know what's going on, and I attend every meeting. I know [policy handled by my committee]; I live with it—I spend ninety per cent of my time on it. But the longer you stay, the more work and understanding and influence you gain, until eventually you become a committee or subcommittee chairman. [Eastern urban leader, Democrat]

As this Congressman testified, seniority offers the individual increased opportunities for exercising leadership in his committee; he may even look forward to assuming a subcommittee chairmanship. The Ritualist is would-be master of the substantive work and procedural maneuver that characterize the House and its specialized work groups, the standing committees. Indeed, the inescapable impression is that the Ritualist role characterizes the institutionally minded Congressman, manifesting what Richard F. Fenno calls the "seniority-protégé-apprentice" system.

The influence of seniority upon purposive roles, however, must be interpreted in the light of additional data. When primary and secondary roles are considered together, the result is an almost exact replica of Table 3-5. But when seniority is analyzed together with party affiliation, one discovers that high seniority is a stimulant for the Ritualist role primarily among Republicans. Less than 20 per cent of the freshman Republicans were Ritualists, compared with 30 per cent of the Democratic newcomers. In both parties Ritualists become more common with greater seniority; and among high-seniority members (six or more terms), Ritualists were found in about equal proportions in both parties.

Another clue to the nature of the Ritualist role is uncovered by examining its relation to formal leadership position in the House.* The relationship is very striking indeed. As Table 3-6 reveals, 57 per cent of the leaders but only 34 per cent of the nonleaders are Ritualists. Tribunes follow the reverse pattern, being more numerous among nonleaders. Variations in the remaining role categories are negligible. The divergence of Ritualists and Tribunes becomes ever clearer when party affiliation and leadership status are considered together, as in Table 3-7.

Table 3-6. Leadership and Primary Purposive Roles Among 116 Members of the House[a]

Purposive Role	Nonleaders	Leaders
Tribune	50%	36%
Ritualist	38	52
Other	12	12
Total	100%	100%
(n)	(74)	(42)

a For analysis of the leadership variable, the two leadership over-samples are included.

These figures permit a summary of our findings thus far: Democrats, whether leaders or not, are more frequently Ritualists than are their Republican counterparts. This partisan variance is especially pronounced among nonleaders. Leaders in both parties, however, demonstrate almost identical patterns of role selection. The existence of a linkage between leadership and the Ritualist role is clear: Leadership responsibilities, or perhaps anticipation

*The definition of House leaders is given in the note on p. 77.

of such responsibilities while the member is awaiting his turn, no doubt foster adherence to the norms associated with the Ritualist conception. Finally, when seniority is considered, nonfreshmen are much more apt to be Ritualists than are freshmen.

Table 3–7. Party, Leadership Position, and Primary Purposive Roles Among 116 Members of the House[a]

Purposive Role	Democrats		Republicans	
	Nonleaders	Leaders	Nonleaders	Leaders
Tribune	42%	38%	62%	33%
Ritualist	42	52	31	52
Inventor	11	5		10
Broker	4	5	3	5
Opportunist			3	
Total	99%	100%	99%	100%
(n)	(45)	(21)	(29)	(21)

a Leadership over-samples included.

The discussion thus far has been confined to background variables (*e.g.*, occupation, political experience) and those political variables (*e.g.*, seniority, leadership) which serve to define the member's position within the House of Representatives. Other politically relevant variables, however, center about the member's formal constituency. Three relatively simple descriptive indicators of Congressional districts will be examined here: region, degree of urbanization,[32] and electoral marginality.* Together with factors internal to Congress, these district characteristics provide a reasonably clear explanation of purposive roles.

In examining purposive roles of members from the four regions, as in Table 3–8, little variation is found from the over-all distribution of roles among the sample (refer to Table 3–2). As might be expected, Ritualists are found most frequently among southerners. The most obvious explanation of this phenomenon is that because of the Democratic party's traditional hegemony in many parts of the South, many of the region's members enter Congress anticipating extended tenure. This constitutes a powerful motivation to concentrate on mastery of legislative procedures and ex-

*This measure, applied to incumbents of the 88th Congress, is based on the members' percentage of the two-party vote in their districts in the prior (1962) elections. Districts where the incumbent received 50.0 to 59.9 per cent of the vote are termed "marginal"; those where the incumbent received more than 60.0 per cent of the vote are termed "safe."

**Table 3–8. Region and Primary Purposive Roles
Among 87 Members of the House**

| | Members From | | | |
Purposive Role	East	South	Midwest	West
Tribune	57%	35%	52%	47%
Ritualist	27	58	43	32
Inventor	5	8		16
Broker	5		5	5
Opportunist	5			
Total	99%	101%	100%	100%
(n)	(21)	(26)	(21)	(19)

pertise in committee business. (And, as noted previously, the Ritualist role seems to be associated as much with *expectation* of seniority as with actual possession of it.) Another reason for playing the Ritualist role could be the relative ease of representing such one-party areas. Fewer Tribunes are found among southerners; and no southerners in the sample are Brokers.

Our southern interviewees are distinctive even when secondary purposive orientations are added to the analysis. The Tribune role has its weakest attraction among southerners ("only" 69 per cent of whom expressed some form of the Tribune focus, compared with 94, 90, and 74 per cent among eastern, midwestern, and western members, respectively). Broker and Opportunist roles are also rarest among southerners. However, the widespread appeal of the Ritualist role somewhat lessens the southerners' distinctiveness in that respect. Secondary Ritualist roles are widespread in all regions except the East, only 43 per cent of whose members expressed the Ritualist role in any form.

The degree of urbanization in a member's district, a factor detailed in Table 3–9, also contributes to our understanding of purposive role. Interestingly enough, members from urban or mixed districts are most likely to be Ritualists. The large number of urban Ritualists is somewhat startling at first glance: high seniority and leadership, associated with the Ritualist role, usually conjure in our minds the image of southern or midwestern members from rural areas. Yet these are not the only Congressmen in the ranks of House elders. Many senior leaders hail from safe urban districts; and such members, mostly Democrats, help account for the relatively high incidence of urban Ritualists. Not so unexpected perhaps is the large proportion of suburban Tribunes. (When secondary roles are counted, fully 91 per cent of the suburbanites are Tribunes.) Suburban districts in the present sample tend to be clustered in the Northeast and far West, and are typically (although not invariably) competitive two-party areas. Thus, the emphasis suburban Congressmen give to the Tribune role is a natural response to political complexity and uncertainty.*

Table 3-9. District Type[a] and Purposive Role Among 87 Members of the House

Purposive Role	Members From			
	Urban	Rural	Suburban	Mixed
Tribune	38%	50%	73%	39%
Ritualist	54	38	9	50
Inventor	8	6	9	6
Broker		6		6
Opportunist			9	
Total	100%	100%	100%	101%
(n)	(24)	(34)	(11)	(18)

a For definition of district type, see note 32 to chap. 3.

The final constituency variable—the degree of electoral competitiveness—shows a rather puzzling relation to purposive roles of the members. Members from competitive districts are slightly more disposed to all purposive roles, except the Inventor role, than their colleagues from safe constituencies. (They articulated an average of 2.2 roles apiece, compared to 1.9 roles for safe members.) Thus, Representatives from marginal districts do not, as might be predicted, shy away from the Ritualist role. And on the other hand, they are only slightly more attracted to the Tribune role than their electorally safe colleagues. This is true in the face of the impact of party affiliation, seniority, and leadership position upon the Ritualist and Tribune roles. However, this finding should not obscure the influence of electoral vulnerability or safety upon role perceptions: indeed, as will be explained in the next chapter, electoral status is the most powerful indicator of a member's style and focus of representation.

*If district type is examined and party affiliation of members held constant, the results parallel the findings presented in Table 3-4 and Table 3-9. That is, regional variations remain within each party; and in every case Republicans tend more often to hold the Tribune role and Democrats the Ritualist role.

In this discussion, purposive role orientations have been examined in light of a series of variables which are relevant to defining the member's status as an individual, a politician, and a participant in an ongoing institution. The most common purposive roles are those of Tribune and Ritualist. They embody the members' most typical orientations to external and internal constituencies respectively. Other purposive roles, though expressed by relatively few members, nonetheless emerged distinctively from the interviews.

Purposive roles would appear to be primarily an outgrowth of the members' socialization in the House. Party affiliation, seniority, and leadership position each appear to have some independent bearing on purposive roles. The Tribune role is most common among low-seniority Republicans, nonleaders, and members from suburban districts in the Northeast or West. The Ritualist role is associated with Democrats of all seniority levels, whether leaders or not. House leaders of both parties show great similarity and tend to be Ritualists rather than Tribunes. In general, the so-called social background variables bear little relation to purposive roles.

MANY TASKS, LITTLE TIME

Purposive role is perhaps the most revealing single indicator we have of how legislators define their jobs. It affords a snapshot of the member's mental image of himself as a legislator. While presumably adjacent to the choices members make in performing their daily tasks, role cognition is not actual behavior in the commonly accepted usage. As an expressed attitude, it is a predisposition to behave in certain ways. This is why the normative quality of role cognition has been stressed: As a self-assessment of what the legislator is *expected* to do, his role cognition will pull him in certain directions and not in others. The Ritualist, for example, would be expected to exhibit somewhat different behavior patterns from a Tribune or holder of another purposive role. Unfortunately, however, few of the more visible choices that a member is called upon to make—in votes, for example—can be linked unambiguously with a given role.

One clue to the member's own job description is the way he budgets his time. From all accounts the twenty-four-hour day has proved far too brief for the modern-day Representative; indeed, "lack of time" is his most frequent complaint.[33] As one member expressed it,

> The biggest problem I have is developing a system of priorities for dealing with the mass of work. The areas of involvement are unlimited. . . . This is a plus factor, but it also leads to frustration. [Midwestern Republican leader, rural district]

Consistent with his notions about what he and others expect, the Congressman must husband his time (and other scarce resources as well) in responding to these varied demands. The member's allocation of time is therefore the outcome of a series of exceedingly difficult personal and political choices. He may discover the tasks he has set for himself are beyond his grasp. So, like the rest of us, he will reshape his expectations to conform roughly with the real world of demands and resources.

The present study permits an indirect analysis of time-budgeting among the sample of Congressmen. Each of the eighty-seven respondents was asked to describe, in detail, the job of the Congressman as he interpreted it. In addition, each was asked to detail the problems he faced in performing his job. From the responses it was possible to identify six major time-consuming activities among which members must allocate their time. Each of the members tended to emphasize one of the six types of activities as the primary time-consuming portion of his job; other activities mentioned were classed as secondary. The results, it should be emphasized, are the respondent's evaluations as expressed in the interview situation and not an audit of his activities over a given time period. Nor do they, of course, tell anything about the time devoted by other people (mainly personal or committee staffs) to projects on the Congressman's behalf. Needless to say, such an audit would be a difficult enterprise; only one study to date has approached this problem on anything approaching a satisfactory scale.[34] Still, the present data provide useful evidence of enacted roles of the respondents, and thus are instructive for the comparisons they permit.

The major time-consuming activities of the eighty-seven members are presented in Table 3-10. General legislative responsibility, including committee work, is clearly perceived by the Congressmen as their most demanding activity. More than three quarters of the respondents indicated that it was their most time-consuming job;

and all but two members found it at least of secondary importance. An audit of the work weeks of 160 members of the 89th Congress, prepared by John S. Saloma, invites a similar interpretation of the Congressional workload. Of the 59 hours put in by the average Congressman each week, nearly two thirds was devoted to legislation, which Saloma concluded was "clearly the dominant concern of the Congressman." The average member, he explains,

> spends an average of 11.1 hours per week on committee work alone and an additional 26.9 hours on the floor, on legislative research and reading, on leadership, and meeting with lobbyists.[35]

Interestingly enough, the typical Congressman assumes the major responsibility (about 60 per cent) in preparing for committee sessions and floor debates, and even does a good portion of his own research (30 per cent). Some individuals deviate considerably from the average: The very senior member or the committee leader may rely primarily on his staff aides; some other members do all their own research.[36] But on the whole, members of the House of Representatives are left to their own devices more frequently than are Senators, who have larger staffs.

Constituency casework—the so-called Errand Boy function—runs a distant second in our survey, although three fourths of the members did count it among their more time-consuming responsibilities. A respected committee chairman gave this colorful description of the Errand Boy function:

> There are a number of secondary jobs—such as "secretary to all the district's Chambers of Commerce," "employment agency" for the district, and "problem analyzer" for disputes between constituents and federal agencies. [Southern Democratic leader, rural district]

Table 3–10. Major Time-Consuming Activities of 87 Members of the House

Activity	Members Listing Activity as Primary	Members Listing Activity as Secondary
Legislator (incl. committee work)	77%	21%
Errand Boy; lawyer for constituents	16	59
Campaigner	2	14
Mentor-Communicator	2	33
Intra-House activity (noncommittee)	2	14
Washington social life		3
Total	99%	154%[a]

a Figures total more than 100 per cent because members listed more than one activity.

In Saloma's study, constituency service accounted for about twenty-eight per cent of the average Representative's work week. This figure would be higher were it not for the fact that much of the burden of constituency casework is normally delegated to the Congressman's personal staff.[37]

Campaigning for re-election was mentioned by surprisingly few of our respondents: Only 2 per cent found it their most time-consuming activity, and for only 14 per cent was it secondary in importance. A related activity is that of Mentor-Communicator. This embraces formal communication with outside publics, including speechmaking, radio and television appearances, and preparation of press releases and newsletters. While the stated purpose of such activity is public enlightenment on issues, much could be classed as a kind of continuous campaigning. Because it advertises the member, such activity serves a surrogate campaign function.[38] Relatively few members gave great emphasis to nonlegislative work on Capitol Hill. And fewer still mention the extracurricular Washington life as important to them.

The emphasis put on legislative work, especially within committees, probably does not surprise anyone who has observed Congress closely. Yet the finding runs counter to the lament, heard often from outside observers and sometimes from Congressmen themselves, that Congressmen have so many distractions that they have little or no time to devote to legislation. One journalist known for astute interpretations of political events argues as follows:

> The main reason . . . that Congress does not legislate better is simply that most Congressmen can no longer afford to regard legislation as the most important part of their jobs.
> Indeed, many of them find it very difficult to sandwich legislative work into the busy schedule of what they describe—correctly—as their more important functions. These relate to their second role, as mediators between their districts and the central government. . . .[39]

Such commentators maintain that Congressmen fall down in their legislative work because of Campaigner and Errand Boy chores. Sometimes reforms are advocated to relieve these burdens;* some-

*Two reform proposals that are typically justified on the grounds that they will free members for legislative work are the Ombudsman or Office of Administrative Counsel (to handle routine constituent casework) and the four-year term (to reduce campaign pressures).

times Congressmen are advised to forget about legislating and concentrate on their other responsibilities.

To be sure, the tension between Legislator and Errand Boy chores is felt by many members of the House. The Congressman, relates Jim Wright (D-Tex.), "realizes that he spends too much of his time on individual requests and too little on his major job of enacting wise legislation and blames himself because he can't figure a way to rearrange this imbalance in his schedule."[40] Undeniably constituency service makes heavy demands upon contemporary legislators. A Republican patriarch described the increased constituency demands he had experienced in several decades on the Hill:

> Today the federal government is far more complex, as is every phase of national life. People have to turn to their Representative for aid. I used to think ten letters a day was a big batch; now I get several hundred a day. In earlier times, constituents didn't know their Congressman's views. With better communications, their knowledge has increased along with their expectation of what he must know. [Eastern Republican leader, mixed district]

One of our respondents explained that he spent 60 per cent of his time on constituent problems but only 20 to 30 per cent on committee meetings and 10 to 20 per cent on floor activities. His ideal time budget, he said, would be 50 per cent for legislative work, 25 per cent for study of major issues, and 25 per cent for communicating with constituents. Others expressed similar frustrations:

> It's a hard way of making a living. You have closer contact with the people than ever before. Constituents are more inclined to express themselves. We have more errand work than before, and less time to do legislative work. [Midwestern Republican leader, rural district]

> I feel the errand boy function is contrary to the Founding Fathers' intent, but it's necessary for election. Glad-handing is degrading but it's desired by constituents. [Southern Democratic nonleader, rural district]

Not all members, however, find constituency work a hindrance to their legislative activities. One senior member claimed he devoted 90 per cent of his time to the work of his key committee. Another, who stated that his committee assignment took half of his time, noted with pride that he regularly read six technical journals to keep abreast of developments. "I spend too much time," he said, "but I am stimulated by it [his committee work]. All the members of the _____ Committee are interested." Other Congressmen insisted that Errand Boy tasks could usually be performed by staff aides; what is required, they said, is skill in organizing staff. Many members, too, feel that the services they perform for constituents are both rewarding and useful. Said one:

> You have to represent your district in contacts with federal agencies. This is often criticized as "errand running," but letters from the district instruct you as to how a program is operating. I don't object to that. [Southern Democratic leader, rural district]

Congressmen clearly have varied reactions to constituency service. Some are openly contemptuous; others learn to delegate large amounts to their staffs. But still others learn to enjoy this aspect of their job, and see it as a unique contribution they can make.

The present data do not exclude the possibility that many members, perhaps very many, encounter severe and sometimes painful conflicts in allocating their time. Every evidence points to the conclusion that Congressmen (like the rest of us) do encounter such conflicts. What the data suggest, however, is that Congressmen have not yet relegated legislative tasks to a subordinate place, either in their purposive conceptions of their jobs or in their budgeting of time. Nor are most Congressmen ready to denigrate the Errand Boy role.

What is of further interest is that the electoral status of the members seems to have little over-all effect upon those activities that they see as most time-consuming. One would assume that members from safe districts could better afford to consider legislation their paramount activity; and that those who are more vulnerable at the polls would concentrate on fence-mending activities—including Errand Boy, Campaigner, and Mentor-Communicator tasks. In fact, the electoral safety of the member's district bears virtually no relation to his primary focus of activities as measured here. In one respect—the incidence of Errand Boy focus—members from safe seats are slightly more constituency-oriented than their colleagues from marginal seats. When secondary time-consuming activities are counted, the results are more nearly as predicted but are still not unambiguous. Mentor-Communicator functions were more often mentioned by respondents from marginal districts in both parties; the Campaigner function was named secondarily more frequently by "marginal" Democrats but not by "marginal" Republicans. And as a secondary focus of activity, Errand Boy functions were named about equally by members from both types of districts. In short, electoral vulnerability does not necessarily condition the activities seen by the members as most time-consuming —a finding that accords with Saloma's conclusion that "constituency . . . bears little direct relationship to the Congressman's time budget."[41] This finding, it will be remembered, also parallels the finding that marginality of district is not strongly associated with purposive role cognitions.

Length of tenure in the House of Representatives is, however, related to the way members spend their time. Briefly summarized, the data presented in Table 3–11 reveal that, once the member possesses some seniority, he is more likely to concentrate on legislative work. Less than sixty per cent of the freshmen named legislation as their primary focus of activity; among second-termers the proportion of Legislators rises considerably; and by the third term it reaches a high plateau. Moreover, all of the nonfreshmen who failed to mention legislative activities as primary at least did so secondarily; in contrast, two freshmen neglected to mention them at all.

Table 3–11. Seniority and Major Time-Consuming Activities of 87 Members of the House

Activity	Members Listing Activity as Primary, by Seniority		
	One Term	2–5 Terms	6–plus Terms
Legislator	59%	83%	79%
Errand Boy	24	11	18
Campaigner	6	3	
Mentor-Communicator	6	3	
Intra-House	6		3
Total	101%	100%	100%
(n)	(17)	(36)	(34)

At the same time, constituency-oriented tasks show an over-all decline among higher-seniority members. Almost one quarter of the freshmen in the sample, for example, are Errand Boys; among second-termers this proportion drops sharply, only to rise gradually among members up to ten terms. No Congressmen having more than ten terms service are Errand Boys. Other constituency-directed functions—Campaigner and Mentor-Communicator—are found mostly among freshmen. In fact, all of those who listed these two categories of activities as primary had served fewer than two full terms in the House at the time of the interviews.

Why, in light of the above, does the proportion of Errand Boys increase slightly among the more senior Congressmen? Of course, it could be that many older members, even if they are (unlike freshman Congressmen) relatively untroubled about re-election, simply enjoy performing casework for constituents. Though some of their colleagues depricate such "busywork," these members relish the prospect of helping individuals. (Incidentally, such chores are normally less demanding intellectually than legislative work.) This explanation is strengthened when the trend is broken down by leadership status as well as seniority. Beyond the second term, the number of Errand Boys among nonleaders rises sharply; indeed, high-seniority nonleaders are more apt to be Errand Boys than any other seniority group (28 per cent versus 24 per cent of the freshmen, for example). In contrast, leaders (all of whom had at least six terms of service) were hardly more likely to be Errand Boys than second- and third-term members. Thus, the slight increase in Errand Boy functions among higher-seniority members is due almost entirely to the frequency of this focus among high-seniority nonleaders.

Further evidence of the influence of intra-House socialization upon the member's focus of activity is found in committee assignments. These all-important work groups differ widely in their work orientations and their attractiveness to members. Though Congressmen may have differing views of the value of a given assignment, Capitol Hill consensus seems to identify the committees on Appropriations, Rules, and Ways and Means as a kind of Holy Trinity of the House.[42] Because competition for these prestigious committees is keen, seats are typically reserved for members with some seniority. To be chosen for membership, moreover, aspirants must usually demonstrate allegiance to the House norm of "doing one's homework." Finally, the workload of these committees is quite demanding (Rules being a possible exception). Most members serving on these committees would thus be expected to appear in the Legislator category. This is the case: 92 per cent of the respondents who were on these three committees gave primary emphasis to legislative work. In contrast, only 76 per cent of the members serving on what are sometimes termed "interest" committees (Agriculture, Education and Labor, Interior, Veterans' Affairs, and Merchant Marine and Fisheries) expressed this orientation. Of the respondents on these committees, 20 per cent were classed as Errand Boys. The data do not permit a detailed comparison of the membership of each House committee, but they do hint that committee assignment, like seniority and leadership status, may be a potent determinant of members' expenditures of time. Saloma is quite emphatic on this point, concluding that "committee assignment, of all the factors examined, appears most directly related to various time budgets."[43]

Finally, as suggested at the outset of this section, members' purposive role orientations should bear a relation to the activities on which they spend the most time. Though the interconnection of the variables cannot be probed satisfactorily because of the small numbers involved, the over-all reasoning is straightforward. The same variables that induce a member to choose a given purposive role also lead him to concentrate on activities appropriate to that role. Selection of a purposive role, moreover, should itself serve as an independent variable, conditioning the member to stress certain activities and avoid others. Our interest centers upon those purposive roles—Tribune and Ritualist—that are present in sufficient numbers to permit generalization. (Though the numbers in the other categories are small, two facts are worthy of notice: The six Inventors are all Legislators, as would be expected; and the lone Opportunist, also as predicted, is a Campaigner.) To obtain a picture of the difference between these two roles, one can compare them with constituency-oriented foci (Errand Boy, Campaigner, and Mentor-Communicator) as well as those encompassing the internal workings of the institution House (Legislator, Intra-House). This has been done in Table 3–12. A large majority of Tribunes and Ritualists, of course, perceive legislative activities as the most time-consuming. However, Ritualists are somewhat more inclined to see lawmaking and other intra-House activities as their primary time-consuming activities. Tribunes, on the other hand, are more apt to mention constituency-oriented activities.

**Table 3–12. Focus of Activity of
Tribunes and Ritualists**

Activity	Tribunes	Ritualists
Legislator	73%	86%
Constituency	27	14
Total	100%	100%
(n)	(41)	(36)

Purposive role is related, at least in these ways, to a member's enacted role. Unfortunately, the precise relationships of variables cannot be ascertained from the data at hand. Do the member's attributes induce him both to express a given purposive role and to engage in activities relevant to that role? Or does the role itself exert an independent influence upon his choice of activities? Presumably both processes are influential.

Compared with the variables discussed thus far, all other factors seem unimportant or derivative in conditioning the member's focus of activity. Some difference can be discerned between the two parties—Democrats more often being Legislators, and Republicans more often stressing constituency-related activities. However, party variance probably stems from the seniority and leadership variables. Democrats in the sample (and in the House generally) have greater average seniority than Republicans; and, being the majority party in the House, Democrats have special leadership responsibilities. As for background variables, these appear to have little relation to the member's focus of activities.

The way a member spends his time, therefore, is in large measure a function of his socialization into the norms and workings of the House. The freshman Congressman, it seems, spends an inordinate amount of time worrying about his district—in many cases, regardless of whether or not he needs to be concerned. Many new members are Errand Boys, Campaigners, or Mentor-Communicators. At the same time, alternative activities are frequently not open to the newcomer. He has much to learn about the procedures and traditions of the House. Very soon he discovers he can accomplish little until he has seniority, information, and his colleagues' respect. His initial committee assignment, moreover, may not be his first preference: He has yet to transfer to a more desirable spot or, failing this, to reconcile himself to his present assignment. Little wonder, then, that so much of the freshman's time is devoted to mending fences at home.

If the Congressman is fortunate enough to get himself re-elected, his attitude toward his work is likely to undergo a rapid transformation. Even a relatively junior legislator can exert some influence on the course of legislation within his committee's jurisdiction. He has familiarity with the House's procedural intricacies, norms, and folkways. He has tested, and been tested by, his fellow members. And of equal significance, he may hope to assume leadership responsibilities—a subcommittee chairmanship perhaps, or floor managership of a bill. The Congressman of moderate seniority, therefore, has many incentives to play the Legislator and relegate constituency work to a secondary place (or at least have more confidence in leaving this work in staff hands). Such members will, of course, encounter roadblocks if they attempt too much or if they try to work against committee elders or party leaders. Indeed, much of the frustration and impatience on Capitol Hill emanates from middle-seniority members whose abilities and ambitions outrun their formal influence. This frustration may induce some members to turn to Errand Boy functions. But there is no doubt that these members have been taught to recognize the paramount place of legislative work. For those in formal leadership posts, the centrality of legislative work is especially marked.

CONCLUSIONS

This discussion has centered on two indicators of the Representative's conception of his responsibilities. The member's purposive role is his normative conception of the ultimate aim of his activities, the "where-from" and "what-for" of the job. Five distinct purposive roles can be identified among our Congressional respondents. Two of these roles—Tribune and Ritualist—are so widely expressed that we may think of them as constituting a generalized job description for the office of U.S. Representative. The remaining purposive roles—Inventor, Broker, and Opportunist—appear distinctly but in fewer numbers.

Perhaps the most striking conclusion to be drawn from our discussion is the broad consensus among members concerning the Tribune and Ritualist components of their jobs. The Tribune is concerned with the classic functions of the legislator-as-representative: he is the spokesman of external constituencies or publics. (The separate issues of *how* members define their spokesmanship and *what* constituencies they are attuned to will be taken up in the following chapter.) The Ritualist is the expert in House business and politics, the "House man." These two roles constitute a sort of grand dualism of orientations, the Outsider and Insider. It is in the nature of the legislator's responsibilities that he is required to play both roles. Traditional representational norms, not to mention the desire to be re-elected, lead to virtual consensus upon the Tribune role. At the same time, common tasks and institutional folkways make inevitable an acceptance of the Ritualist orientation. Invariably the Representative is poised between these externally and internally based norms, which underscores the mediate character of the legislature as a group of fiduciary bargainers.

The consensual nature of the Tribune-Ritualist duality minimizes the extent to which members may be differentiated from one another through their emphasis on one or the other orientation. However, by identifying the one role that appears to have greatest weight in each respondent's mind, we have been able to identify certain distinctive characteristics of the holders of various purposive conceptions. In general, we have found the so-called "social background" variables of little importance—though certain derivative differences do appear. Nor does ideological predisposition offer much explanation of purposive orientation. (Interestingly, the Inventors—who might be thought of as the "agitators" of the legislative arena—are the only ideologically distinct role grouping.) Internal House norms and formal leadership positions are positively related to the Ritualist conception. Thus, we have seen that Ritualists tend to be Democrats, leaders, and members who have some seniority (or expectation of seniority). Because such members tend to represent certain kinds of districts, they show distinctive characteristics in location and degree of urbanization of their electoral bases. A slight occupational difference, also primarily derivative, was also noted between Tribunes and Ritualists.

A second indicator of purposive orientation is what we have called focus of activity. This measure pertains to the *proportion of members* who list each activity as most time-consuming, not to the *proportion of time* each member devotes to each activity. Our findings, however, parallel those reported by Saloma (who employed the latter measure). Focus of activity, moreover, appears to bear some relationship to purposive role, though whether this relation is an independent one cannot be ascertained.

Two conclusions can be drawn from an examination of members' focus of activity. First, the large majority of Representatives devote the greatest portion of their time and energies to legislative work. A significant minority, however, emphasize the so-called Errand Boy functions and other constituency-oriented tasks. Second, like purposive roles, focus of activity is in large measure a function of the member's socialization into the tasks and norms of the House. Congressmen with more than a single term of service are more likely to be Legislators than are freshmen. And within the seniority ranks, leadership position also tends to draw the member toward Legislator functions and away from Errand Boy functions. Committee assignment also plays a part. Other variables either seem unimportant or derivative.

Taken together, these two measures—purposive role and focus of activity—are the broadest indicators we have of Congressmen's job definitions. Quite obviously, however, the job embraces many other role subsets through which he relates himself to specific "others" in his environment—including constituents, his party and its leaders, lobbyists, the Administration, and colleagues in the House. A complete audit of these role subsets cannot be attempted, for it would embrace virtually the entire scope of the members' personal and political lives. The following two chapters, however, will consider several role subsets that are of theoretical and practical relevance in understanding legislative behavior. Chapter 4 will be devoted to the roles that Congressmen play in dealing with constituents and their claims. Orientations toward political party and the claims of interest groups will then be explored in Chapter 5.

CHAPTER 4

THE CONGRESSMAN AS REPRESENTATIVE

R epresentation is one of the most pervasive and important processes of political life. It is found in virtually all political structures: In our own political system, for example, representative qualities have been claimed for such diverse political actors as Presidents[1] and bureaucrats.[2] But it is the elected legislator who has been the focus of most normative and empirical inquiries into the nature of representation. The special fiduciary relationship of the legislator to the sovereign electorate was a foundation for classical doctrines of legislative supremacy, as enunciated by John Locke and others.[3] At least one political scientist, moreover, has argued forcefully that representation is the key to the much-discussed decline of Congress. "Congress has lost power," writes Samuel Huntington, "because it has . . . defects as a representative body."[4]

Members of the U.S. House of Representatives place great emphasis on the task of representation. As we saw in Chapter 3, the role of Tribune was the dominant purposive orientation among our respondents. No fewer than eighty-two per cent of the members interviewed manifested some form of this role—either with a primary or subsidiary emphasis. One may further observe that the respondents placed somewhat greater weight upon roles relevant to representation (Broker and Opportunist, as well as Tribune) than upon roles directed to the internal workings of Congress (Inventor, and especially Ritualist). Whether this pattern has, or will, remain constant is uncertain. Clearly, however, tradition, democratic norms, and voters' expectations have conspired to give representation a central place in the legislator's conception of his tasks.

As seems true of all key concepts, however, representation is more easily discussed than defined. Traditional debates on the subject have been premised on an understanding of representation as a *status:* the concordance of two separate and definable qualities, the will of the represented and the behavior of representatives. Alfred de Grazia has described representation as "a condition which exists when the characteristics and acts of one vested with public functions are in accord with the desires of one or more persons to whom the functions have objective or subjective importance."[5] Such a definition unfortunately raises a number of crucial questions concerning the terms or variables involved in representation. How, for example, should the "desires" of constituencies be measured? On the other hand, what "characteristics" or "acts" of decision-makers can be taken as indicators of representation, and how can they be measured?

Notwithstanding formidable problems of measurement, a number of techniques have been employed by social scientists in probing the representative attributes of political decision-makers. Following de Grazia's terminology, an audit may be taken of the decision-makers' "characteristics"—their social backgrounds and formal associations.[6] The occupational or demographic peculiarities of legislative bodies, of the kind discussed in Chapter 2, have frequently been marshalled as indicators of the representational capacities of members. Further, the public choices of decision-makers may be cataloged and compared with these background or constituency characteristics.[7] Such techniques rest on inferences that can presumably be drawn from the "accord" between demographic characteristics and patterns of decision-making.

Definitions of representation as a status are open to conceptual as well as methodological objection. What behavioral processes are at work when decision-makers are "in accord with" their constituencies? The concept of status can do little more than assume these political or psychological processes. Thus, it seems more valid conceptually to think of representation in terms of a *process* (or processes), rather than in the more conventional manner. James Wilson, in this as in so many other ways one of the most foresighted of our Founding Fathers, defined representation as the chain of communication between the people and those to whom they have committed the important charge of exercising the delegated powers necessary for the administration of public affairs. This chain may consist of one link, or more links than one, but it should always be sufficiently strong and discernible.[8]

Another helpful definition has been offered by Seymour M. Lipset, who sees representation as a *system of actions* that serves to "facilitate interchange between authority and the spontaneous groupings of society," a system that includes "most major attempts to influence authoritative decisions."[9] In this view, representation is a process of interaction between social groupings and political decision-makers. The forms of interaction are highly varied. Often they are carefully organized or planned, as in an electoral campaign or interest-group lobbying; but there is also a large margin for relatively spontaneous interaction. This concept of representation leads inevitably to one of the most central problems with which political scientists must deal: the definition and measurement of influence.

One strategy of research that brings the student very close to the representational process itself is the study of decision-makers' attitudes, or predispositions, toward influence-bearing stimuli. One possible approach is a comprehensive audit of communication cues received by the decision-makers.[10] Though rarely implemented because of severe data-gathering requirements, this technique rests on James Wilson's assumption that communication is a crucial ingredient of the process of representation (and indeed of influence generally). Another technique for uncovering the processes of influence has been demonstrated by Raymond A. Bauer and his associates, who marshaled a variety of data to probe the effectiveness of business lobbying on the tariff question in the 1950's.[11] Yet another variation on these approaches has been reported by Warren E. Miller and Donald E. Stokes. In an imaginative combination of interviews with Congressmen, survey research in their districts, and analysis of their voting records in Congress on selected issues, Miller and Stokes were able to chart the "paths of influence" leading from constituent attitudes to voting choices in Congress, via the perceptions of the representative himself.[12] Among other things, they discovered that the paths of influence varied with the saliency of the issues to the electorate.

Role analysis offers another method of approaching the representational process. Because the Congressman's roles constitute his normative expectations—*e.g.*, "How should I, as a legislator, respond or behave toward X or Y?"—they indicate his predisposition to react in certain ways to stimuli. In this view the Congressman-as-representative is an individual who assumes certain roles in dealing with persons or groups making demands upon him. Quite obviously, such claims are made in diverse ways (structured or unstructured) by a wide range of relevant "others" —including constituents, lobbyists, party leaders, or Administration spokesmen. The Congressman-as-representative is a composite of the roles he takes in these varied settings, and on different questions, toward his diverse claimants. Rather than attempt the impossible task of a comprehensive audit, we have opted to analyze several generalized role dimensions that can suggest the member's responses in a wide variety of circumstances. In this chapter, two broad dimensions of representational roles are examined: the member's *style* and *focus* of representation.[13] In the chapter to follow, role orientations toward two important classes of claimants, political party and interest groups, will be studied.

REPRESENTATIONAL STYLE

Although Congressmen display surprising consensus on the importance of representing external constituencies, they differ widely in their styles of performing this function. The central stylistic difference revolves around the question of whether the member sees himself as following his own knowledge or conscience in making choices, or whether he views himself as following "instructions" (either actual or implied) from his constituents. Instructions may be explicitly conveyed to the Representative, limiting either his policy choices or his conduct. Or they may be absorbed by the member to the point that he is capable of anticipating reactions to his behavior, even in the absence of formal communication.[14] Indeed, the instructions may be so internalized that the decision-maker himself is convinced he is acting upon his own premises.

Conversely, the legislator may actually accept "instructions" from sources other than external constituencies. In order to reduce to manageable proportions the complex issues before him, the contemporary legislator frequently searches out cues from persons or groups having little if anything to do with constituents: from colleagues or committee experts, for example, or from an informed consensus on an issue or problem. In fact, it has been discovered that influence-bearing communications on Capitol Hill most frequently circulate *internally* among the members themselves and their staff aides.[15] By acting upon such cues, the legislator is able to avoid the virtually impossible assignment of informing himself directly about each issue before making a choice.

Yet the stylistic distinction has enormous consequences, both empirical and normative, for the process of representation. Thus it has remained an important and fascinating issue for observers since the rise of modern legislative institutions. The traditional point of departure is Edmund Burke's classic dictum that a legislator should act as a trustee for "the general reason of the whole [community]," rather than the spokesman for "local purposes . . . [and] local prejudices."[16] Burke's point of view has always had its admirers; and legislators who have displayed courage in adhering to their own conception of the public interest in the face of contrary public sentiment have often times been treated kindly by historical hindsight.[17] This norm of behavior remains embodied in many constitutional provisions, especially in parliamentary systems. It is probable that members of the contemporary House of Commons view their deliberative tasks (to the extent that they engage in such tasks at all) primarily in terms of the Burkean Trustee.* In colonial Virginia, perhaps the most English of the American colonies, members of the House of Burgesses came close to Burke's ideal.†

Yet in democratic polities the Burkean ideal is often hazardous. Burke himself was eventually turned out of office for his candor; and for all but six years (1774–1780) he owed his seat in Parliament to the patronage of the Marquis of Rockingham. What came to be referred to as the "Burkean concept" of the legislator-as-trustee was abhorrent to theorists of majoritarian democracy, such

---

*The author's interviews with a sample of M.P.'s in 1966 pointed unmistakably to this conclusion. Voting in the Commons is, of course, overwhelmingly along party lines. But most members engage in lobbying, both within their parties and with the government of the day. In these activities, it seems clear that the Trustee style predominates.[18]

†An explanation has been offered by Daniel J. Boorstin: "Virginia was governed by its men of property. . . . The voters . . . had just enough power to prevent the irresponsibility of their representatives, but not enough to secure their servility."[19]

as the Abbé Sieyés, Thomas Paine, and James Mill. They viewed the legislature (in Mill's words) as a "congress of ambassadors from different . . . interests" and exercised great ingenuity in devising ways of holding representatives accountable to these interests.[20]

Contemporary electorates, motivated by understandable self-interest and conditioned by democratic norms, seem to expect their legislators to follow their instructions rather than exercise independent judgment.[21] In 1967, Representative Lee H. Hamilton (D-Ind.) inquired in a constituent survey how he should decide to vote on various issues. Of the 7,474 constituents who replied to the question, 69 per cent said the Congressman should "vote according to the majority wishes of the district as he interprets those wishes"; 31 per cent felt he should "vote according to . . . conscience and judgment."[22]* Economic and social groupings, moreover, tend to evaluate Congressional performance in light of "what Congress has done for us lately."[23] These conclusions are mitigated by the fact that few issues are salient, much less visible, to any given grouping of voters. It is primarily in a handful of policy areas which meet these criteria that the electorate demands its instructions be followed.[24]

In fact, the Burkean conception tends to confuse the issue of representational *style* ("instructions" versus "judgment") with the issue of *focus* ("local purposes" versus "general good"). Though closely related, the two dimensions are not conterminous. It is entirely possible, and indeed not unlikely considering contemporary legislative recruitment patterns, for a Congressman to be a Burkean and a parochial at one and the same time. That is, constituent instructions have the quality of personal judgment because the member is at heart a transplanted constituent. In the present survey, for example, fifty-nine per cent of the respondents agreed with the statement "I seldom have to sound out my constituents because I think so much like them that I know how to react to almost any proposal."

Conversely, it has been argued persuasively that Burke himself was not the Trustee he is assumed to have been, but rather a Delegate who happened to be responsive to the national constituency.[25] In his view, and in the historic British view, Parliament

---

*In such questionnaires (and in general), Congressmen tend to hear from those who agree with them. However, this bias would seem less relevant to the validity of a nonissue question such as the above.

was an immediate embodiment of the constituent parts of the realm, both Lords and Commons. Therefore, the constitution and not the electorate was the motivating and legitimizing force behind the legislative body. More recently former Senator Paul H. Douglas (D-Ill.) expressed the rationale behind the Burkean representative role:

> I wanted to represent the general public interest. It is frequently not represented. The power Establishment in the Senate is on the whole biased against the public interest. The small taxpayers— people of low income; of minority groups—are individually weak. The special interests, producing interests, are . . . organized. In the struggle between concentrated private interest and diffused general interest, the private interests have all the resources and drive they need to win.[26]

In Douglas' interpretation (and probably in Burke's), the public interest is the aggregate of many specific interests that would, in his view, be overlooked in a legislature based solely on electoral recruitment.

Thus, more than a single dimension is involved in the traditional distinction between the Burkean Trustee and the instructed Delegate. One dimension has to do with the legislator's *style* of representation: whether, in our terminology, he accepts instructions (Delegate), proceeds by his own lights (Trustee), or acts on some combination of the two (Politico). The other dimension is his *focus* of representation: whether the legislator's referent is primarily the whole nation (Burke's "mystic corpus"), his geographic constituency, a nongeographic interest-grouping, or some combination of these. In reality Congressmen may employ several or all of these roles as the situation demands; but, as in most discussions of role-taking, the roles to be described here are members' generalized orientations to demands made upon them.

The distribution of representational styles among eighty-seven of the Congressmen interviewed is shown in Table 4-1. Half of the respondents expressed either the pure Trustee or Delegate conceptions, and were fairly evenly divided between the two. Almost half of the sample, however, fell somewhere between these extremes—that is, the Politico role. And if a simple index is constructed from the continuum represented by the three role types, the average "style index" score for the entire sample is 1.99 (on a scale of 3.0), almost squarely on the Politico role.*

Table 4–1. Distribution of Representational Styles Among 87 Members of the House of Representatives

Trustee	28%
Politico	46
Delegate	23
Undetermined	3
Total	100%
(n)	(87)
Style Index	1.99

Trustees cherish their independence from outside pressures, whether from constituents or from organized interests. Though they concede the necessity of communicating their judgments to outside publics, they resist the notion that they should forfeit ultimate judgment on issues. Consider the following statements of Trustees in our sample:

> The Founding Fathers intended us to exercise our own judgment, not to weigh mail. I have no hesitation in telling my constituents why I vote the way I do. [Eastern Republican leader, rural district]

> My job . . . can usually be accomplished . . . despite heavy pressures from various constituents. This type of pressure seldom bothers me; I am not here to reflect the wishes of any one individual or group, but rather to make the right decisions and then to explain them to my constituents. [Western Democratic leader, suburban district]

> Our legislative system is premised on the belief that we are going to elect qualified people to represent us in Washington. However, we often see highly qualified people defeated on votes that are of little or no national importance. That is unfortunate.
> . . . A Congressman doesn't lead the people. He tells them which direction he wants to go and then goes there. If the people don't like that direction, it is their option to go the other way. It is important that a Congressman delineate clearly his views, but he shouldn't have to go back to the people. [Midwest Republican nonleader, rural district]

*A simple "style index" score was assigned to each respondent on the following basis: Trustee, 3; Politico, 2; Delgate, 1. Index scores were then averaged for the population in question—in this case, the total sample of 84. (Three respondents whose role could not be ascertained were omitted).

Many Congressmen who are not Trustees still stress the ideal of independent judgment. An overwhelming majority of the members—including those expressing diverse styles and foci of representation—expressed agreement with the proposition that "A Congressman ought to decide how to vote on most issues by asking himself if the proposed law is morally right." By the same token, sixty-eight per cent of our interviewees *disagreed* with the statement that "A Representative ought to work for what his constituents want, even though this may not always agree with his personal views."

The Trustee role is not necessarily unrealistic, given citizen apathy or ignorance on many issues legislators must cast votes upon. For an expression of the independence felt by some legislators, it is hard to improve on the remarks of one of Lewis A. Dexter's respondents, the late Herman Eberharter (D-Pa.):[27]

> You know, I am sure you will find out a Congressman can do pretty much what he decides to do and he doesn't have to bother too much about criticism. I've seen plenty of cases since I've been up here where a guy will hold one economic or political position and get along all right; and then he'll die or resign and a guy comes in who holds quite a different . . . position and he gets along all right too. That's the fact of the matter.

When asked to react to a paraphrase of the above statement, forty-two per cent of the respondents in the present study expressed their agreement. Many others, while not believing their constituents so lenient, assume the Trustee role anyway.

The opposing sentiment, that of the Delegate, was expressed by one of our respondents as follows:

> The most important thing I do is to represent my people. Ideally, they should have a voice in the government. Yet actually, they only have a voice at times—it is just impossible for them to make their wishes heard. . . . I am a realist, though, and I know that I can't do everything for everyone. [Southern rural nonleader, Democrat]

The Delegate rationalizes his position through a rigid application of the principle of popular sovereignty—the notion that the people should have their way even if their elected representative thinks otherwise. Though not as widespread among members as the notion of independent judgment, this norm nonetheless has firm roots in democratic political theory. Of our respondents, 32 per cent agreed that "A Representative ought to work for what his constituents want even though this may not always agree with his personal views." And while only 13 per cent of the Trustees agreed with the statement, the Delegates were split evenly on the question.

The Delegate role was the least frequently articulated by our respondents. In this respect at least, the present findings are consonant with those in the four state legislatures examined by Wahlke and his associates. However, the proportion of Delegates in the House is higher than in any of these states; and in surveying legislatures in three additional states, Pennsylvania, Wisconsin, and North Carolina, other investigators found a plurality of Delegates.[28]

The present data do not, however, support the further speculation by Wahlke and his colleagues that "the trustee role is the easiest and the delegate role the most difficult to take."[29] A large plurality of Congressmen—close to half of the entire sample—express *both* Trustee and Delegate conceptions. This hybrid role has been termed Politico. In very many cases, respondents evidenced sophisticated thinking concerning the kinds of choices for which they can play the role of Trustee and those for which the Delegate role is appropriate or expected. Many Congressmen observe that their problem is one of balancing the one role against the other. Almost by definition, this stratagem is a more demanding response than either of the two "pure" stylistic orientations. Politicos in our sample, for example, were more likely than holders of the other roles to agree that "So many groups and individuals want so many different things that it is often difficult to know what stand to take."

The following expressions illustrate the varied permutations of the Politico orientation:

> I have to vote the way I think right. I like to think the constituency thinks the same way. By and large, principle is the criterion. On minor issues, I can go along with the constituency. Generally, people think the same way in my area. [Southern Democratic nonleader, rural district]

> I would mix the roles of representation, especially in areas where I am knowledgeable. There is an educational function when the Congressman's role differs from that of the constituent—for example, foreign aid and military affairs. On broad issues, I try to reflect the attitude of the constituency—not necessarily that of pressure groups, but of the average person. I do like to sample

every two years to find out views on broad issues. [Midwest Republican leader, mixed district]

[The Congressman] must remember his district but he must also vote as he personally sees fit on an issue. There is a balance which each Congressman works out between these two factors which defies definition in any succinct manner. [Western Democratic nonleader, rural district]

Some legislators, following Edmund Burke's example, explicitly link their stylistic approach to representation with specifically defined constituencies, as in the following comment:

There is a heavy responsibility to represent the people of the district and the country at large, . . . both [to] make your own decisions and to represent [others]. [Southern Republican non-leader, rural district]

Politicos express themselves in a great variety of ways, and their stylistic approach is clearly the dominant one in the House. By contrast, in the state legislatures that have been studied this role was clearly subordinate, commanding allegiance from no more than twenty-nine per cent of the respondents (in Ohio).

The Politico role is a natural response to the conflicting demands made upon legislators. "Both the shifting political demands and the finely balanced equities of choice," Sorauf writes, "force [the legislator] to choose only tentatively and cautiously, one issue at a time." [30] The Politico, moreover, fulfills the normative requirements of the fiduciary function. The fiduciary must act independently in his constituent's interest, even when the constituent is unaware or uninformed on the issue. At the same time the fiduciary must not normally violate the constituent's wishes. [31]

Fortunately for the Congressman, his constituents speak with a clear voice on relatively few issues. Most legislation affects a given constituency only indirectly; and in any event the threshold of public information and understanding of issues is quite low. [32] This is particularly true for the increasing number of issues that are intricate and technical.* The member must frequently search out other cues or premises upon which to base his choices on such matters.

*This characteristic of modern government is suggested by Wahlke and his colleagues as an explanation for the frequency with which the Trustee role appeared in state legislatures. They argue further that, because issues have become more complex with time, the Trustee role has probably grown in importance while the Delegate role has declined. Further research is undoubtedly needed on this point, perhaps through content analyses of legislative debates or biographical materials.

On the other hand, the interviews imply that the late Representative Eberharter somewhat overstated the extent to which members feel free to act independently of constituent interests or demands. Perhaps the Representatives are simply voicing the strong democratic norm that accords sovereignty to their electorate. Or perhaps they overestimate the sanctions their constituents are willing or able to invoke. Nonetheless most members are keenly aware that constituencies impose certain boundaries on their activities. When these boundaries are trespassed, as sometimes happens, the member may face increased opposition in campaigning for re-election, or even the ultimate sanction of electoral defeat. Thus, many Congressmen are hypersensitive to anticipated constituent reaction, regardless of the real threat that may be involved.*

FOCUS OF REPRESENTATION

Related to representational style but distinct from it is the dimension of representational focus: that is, the particular constituency or constituencies that serve as referents for the legislator's behavior. The distinction between style and focus has already been pointed out in discussing Edmund Burke's classic statement. However one interprets Burke's prescribed style of representation, it is clear that he viewed the legislator as responding to national rather than localized interests. Even in the eighteenth century, Burke's position must have appeared somewhat uncompromising. Whether beholden to the local gentry (as in the so-called "rotten boroughs") or to a more broadly based electorate (as in the Bristol constituency), members of Parliament ignored localized interests only at the risk of defeat. Democratic theory of the nineteenth century tended to underscore the legitimacy of localized demands. It was probably only with the rise of party loyalty that this situation was modified for the average member of Parliament.[34]

An important characteristic of American Congressmen is that they are elected from local geographic constituencies. District

*On the basis of his interviews with Congressmen concerning the tariff question (epitomized by the Eberharter statement), Dexter reasoned that legislators were freer of constituency pressures than is generally assumed. This is undoubtedly a valid point, and constitutes an important corrective for traditional assumptions. What is argued here, however, is that, for whatever reason, this fact does not persuade most legislators to assume the risks of expressing the premise.[33]

electoral contests are affected by national voting trends, but the extent of the effect differs greatly from region to region and from district to district.[35] The localist character of campaigns and elections is reinforced by recruitment patterns that favor locals and discourage carpetbaggers—the formal requirement, for example, that Representatives reside in the state from which they are elected, and informal norms that encourage candidates long associated with their districts.[36] It is not surprising, therefore, that localism is viewed by many observers as a dominant characteristic of Congress, and especially the House; and that Congressional critics have frequently faulted the locally based legislator's tunnel-vision in confronting broad questions of national policy. There seems to be general agreement with Rosenau's conclusion that Congressmen, as "segmental" leaders, "give highest priority to the subnational units which they head or represent."[37]

This conclusion—that legislators are more frequently parochial than national in constituency focus—is borne out, though with important qualifications, by the present sample of Congressmen. The representational foci expressed by eighty-seven respondents are shown in Table 4-2. Responses in which the district focus appeared predominant formed a large plurality; and on the index constructed along the national-district continuum, the entire sample had an average somewhat to the district end,* corroborating Wil-

Table 4–2. Distribution of Representational Foci Among 87 Members of the House

Nation dominant	28%
Nation and district equal	23
District dominant	42
Nongeographic	5
Undetermined	3
Total	101%
(n)	(87)
Focal Index	1.84

*A simple index score was assigned to each respondent on the following basis: nation dominant, 3; nation-district equal, 2; district dominant, 1. Respondents with a nongeographic focus were placed with the second (nation-district equal) group. Then index scores were averaged for the population in question—in this case, the total sample of 84. (Three respondents whose role could not be determined were omitted.)

liam S. White's impression that Locals comprise the largest single grouping of Congressmen.[38]

Locals rest their case on the Constitutional importance of individual constituencies in the House of Representatives. Thus, they are more inclined than other members to accept the proposition that "A Representative ought to work for what his constituents want even though this may not always agree with his personal views." (Of the Locals, 41 per cent agreed with the statement, compared to 30 per cent of those manifesting a combined national-district focus and only 11 per cent of those with a pure national focus.) And they are somewhat more apt to voice the Errand Boy function of constituency service. (The statement was: "An important part of a Congressman's job should be to go to bat for constituents in their dealings with executive agencies." Of the Locals, 84 per cent agreed, compared with 61 per cent of the Nationals.)

The amalgam of local interests, Locals contend, produces a fair approximation of the public interest. As one localist member explained,

> I am a purist. I feel that a House member's job is to represent the people back home. For example, the only four wet-corn growers in the country are in my district, and I am their sole voice. Likewise, the date growers should be represented only by *their* Congressman; the salmon industry should be able to count on Pacific Northwest Congressmen, and so forth. I might concur with Representative X from Anywhere for the good of the country, but my primary responsibility must always be [my] district.
>
> A Representative is interested primarily with his own little piece of land. A combination of the actions of all Congressmen creates, in effect, House policy. [Midwestern Republican nonleader, rural district]

Again, Locals stress that conflicts between the district and their other constituencies do not usually materialize: What is good for the district is good for others as well.

> My job is to serve the best interests of my district as well as the best interests of the nation. There is not conflict here, because whatever is good for a segment of the country is good for the whole. [Southern Democratic leader, rural district]

Some respondents who conceded the primacy of local interests, however, were also critical of it. As one expressed himself,

> Members of Congress are too parochial in their views. They
> tend to represent only their district, when they should represent
> the state and the nation as well. [Western urban nonleader,
> Democrat]

Such comments only serve to strengthen the conclusion, gained
from a careful analysis of the interviews, that for a large plurality
of Congressmen the local district stands as the primary referent.

This strong local strain among members should not, however,
be construed as unalloyed parochialism. Many respondents, though
their comments displayed a district focus, nonetheless evidenced
considerable concern for, and knowledge of, problems and issues
transcending district boundaries. Not even the most archetypical
Local can avoid devoting some attention to extraconstituency
decision premises—if only to search out and accept the judgments
of experts before voting on these questions.

> Everything I do has a relationship to the district, but it's not the
> only basis for choice. [Midwestern Republican nonleader, rural
> district]

Slightly more than half (51 per cent) of the respondents give *at
least* equal emphasis in their comments to the notion of the "larger"
constituency. This number includes members who appear to give
equal weight to national and district claims as well as those (28
per cent) who clearly manifest a national orientation. These figures
underscore the fact that Congressmen display a variety of constituency perspectives.

Of particular interest is the small group of members whose role
focus is not strictly geographic in character. The constituencies
to which these members are attuned are best described by referring
to some of their comments—of which the following are typical:

> My constituency is not just my district, but Negroes everywhere.
> [Northern urban leader, Democrat]

> Now, I am exerting every pressure to pass civil rights legisla-
> tion—as a matter of justice, and because the future of the nation is
> tied to civil rights. . . . My district is diversified—fifty per cent
> Negro and Puerto Rican, and the balance Italian, Jewish, and so
> forth. To some extent this means that I represent all pro-civil-
> rights people in the United States. [Northern urban nonleader,
> Democrat]

> I'm not just a member from a district. I'm chairman of a com-
> mittee with _____ staff members and a big responsibility to Ameri-

can [names important producer interest]. . . . I have to look out for the _____, their welfare—solve their problems. . . . After my committee responsibility, I've got to look after my district's interests and problems. [Southern rural leader, Democrat]

As can be seen from these comments, this role orientation cannot easily be located on the district-national continuum. Nongeographic focus, to be sure, harmonizes in every case with the interests of the respondent's district. It is hardly surprising, for example, that the member from a mixed racial and ethnic area perceives his district as a microcosm of the larger civil rights conflict of the 1960's. Nevertheless, the nongeographic focus is undeniably broader than the member's own district. In each case the member espouses the concerns of a substantive interest-grouping that is widely scattered geographically. In the cases of the two leaders quoted above—both of whom are committee chairmen—these generalized constituencies are clienteles of their legislative committees. Clearly the focus of such members contains both district and supradistrict elements. For purposes of further analysis, therefore, these respondents are classed with those expressing an equal national-district emphasis.

The distribution of constituent focus is consistent with the findings of Wahlke and his associates concerning legislators in the three states for which they were able to gather reliable information (California, New Jersey, and Ohio).[39] In each state a plurality (in one case a majority) of the respondents identified primarily with their local electoral districts. The proportion of respondents indicating a statewide focus was considerably smaller. The similarity of results among respondents at two institutional levels of our political system does not, of course, suggest that the psychological processes involved in area focus are necessarily identical.

Style and focus of representation are closely associated. The correlation is demonstrated by the figures in Table 4-3. That these two dimensions are highly correlated—as might be expected—tends to support Burke's intuition, if not his logic, in mixing the two. Indeed, many Congressmen fuse the two dimensions, as evidenced in the previously cited comment of one respondent:

> There is a heavy responsibility to represent the people of the district and the country at large, . . . both [to] make your own decisions and to represent [others]. [Southern rural nonleader, Republican]

Table 4–3. Relationship of Representational Style and Focus Among 81 Members of the House

Focus	Style		
	Trustee	Politico	Delegate
National	73%	33%	
Natl.-dist.	18	33	10%
District	9	33	90
Total	100%	99%	100%
(n)	(22)	(39)	(20)
Focal Index	2.54	2.03	1.10

There is every reason to expect that the Trustee, who makes choices on the basis of conscience, appraisal of facts, and so forth, would be inclined to turn his primary attention away from his own district. Conversely, the Delegate—who makes decisions on the basis of "instructions"—would be inclined (at least under a locally based recruitment system) to look to his electorate as the source of those instructions.

That these two dimensions, stylistic and focal, are not entirely redundant is evident also from Table 4–3. A few members are found outside the "normal" patterns (*i.e.*, Trustee-National and Delegate-District). Members appearing in the middle of one dimension (*i.e.*, Politicos or equal District-National focus), moreover, can usefully be differentiated along the other dimension. It remains to identify and analyze some of the variables associated with representational roles.

THE POLITICAL ENVIRONMENT OF REPRESENTATION

What influences a legislator's style or focus of representation? This question is both inevitable and perplexing. Our empirical curiosity and our desire to render normative judgments require that we learn more about the conditions under which legislators make choices. Yet, as we have cautioned, role cognitions are not themselves behaviors in the common sense of the term, but rather predispositions to behave in certain patterned ways. On a more mundane level, our inquiry (like many similar elite studies) is constricted by a limited sample-size—a factor that virtually precludes sophisticated multivariate analysis. These problems should be borne in mind as we try to search out the sources of representational role orientations.

Our data nonetheless yield several insights into the question we have posed. At least the general outline of the findings is unmistakable; and the details, while not clear enough to be discerned with certainty, can still be traced tentatively. The conclusions are generally consistent with our intuitive understanding of the problem, and with much of the prior research on the question. In some instances, moreover, the findings enable us to clarify and extend our knowledge.

Even the barest intuition would lead us to suggest that the Representative's electoral fortunes would figure significantly in his selection of a style or focus of representation. In particular, members elected from competitive two-party areas should display different representational roles than colleagues elected from safe one-party areas. Any simple measure of party competitiveness, unfortunately, is bound to conceal subtle differences among individual districts. For present purposes, the very simplest measure has been selected. Those districts where the incumbent was returned by 50.0 to 59.9 per cent of the two-party vote in the preceding election (1962) were classed as "marginal," while those returning the incumbent by more than 60.0 per cent of the vote were considered "safe."[40] This measure tends to underestimate those districts where incumbents of a single party win consistently though by modest percentages; but it is accurate enough to serve the purpose here.*

Style and focus of representation are largely a reflection of the amount of electoral uncertainty that the member faces at the polls. As he assesses the level of competition he is likely to face at the polls, so the Congressman tends to weigh the importance of others' claims upon his behavior. The basic evidence for this conclusion appears in Table 4–4, which reveals in dramatic fashion the impact of this variable. Among respondents from safe districts, 35 per cent were Trustees, and only 11 per cent were Delegates; while 19 per cent of the marginal members were Trustees, and 44 per cent were Delegates. Representational focus varies equally strongly with the district's vote. Of the safe members, 34 per cent are Nationals and 38 per cent Locals; but among marginal members, the percentages were 19 per cent and 53 per cent respectively. In both instances the relationships are statistically significant;

*Except for the problem mentioned, the 1962 classification was confirmed in every case by the 1960 election results and seemed to conform with the results of prior years, where those were available.

and in both instances the simple index scores we have constructed
reflect the impact of the constituency variable.

Table 4–4. Marginality of District and Representational Roles Among 87 House Members

Style	District Type [a] Marginal	Safe	Focus	District Type Marginal	Safe
Trustee	19%	35%	National	19%	34%
Politico	37	54	Natl.-dist.[b]	28	29
Delegate	44	11	District	53	38
Total	100%	100%	Total	100%	101%
(n)	(32)	(52)	(n)	(32)	(53)
Style Index	1.75	2.24	Focal Index	1.66	1.98

a "Marginal districts are defined as those in which the incumbent won re-election by less than 60 per cent of the vote in the November 1962 Congressional election. Safe districts are those in which the member polled 60 per cent or more of the vote.

b Includes 8 per cent nongeographic focus.

The importance of electoral margin is not surprising, for in
many ways this is the first fact of political life with which legislators must come to terms. First and most fundamentally, survival
depends on re-election: "You can't be a statesman unless you get
elected." Secondly, the margin of victory undoubtedly serves the
member as an indicator of the amount of "breathing space" he
is to be allowed in the performance of his job. Many Congressmen read election results this way and respond accordingly. They
may exaggerate their peril, but clearly the most recent election
can serve as a psychological monitor. Nor is electoral defeat the
legislator's only fear: A downturn in electoral support may constitute a very real psychological threat, and may invite vigorous
challenges in the primary or general election. For such members
the problem is not whether they win or lose but whether their
margin remains comfortable. Finally, the same factors that render
a district safe for one party or the other may also make it easier
to represent. That is, one-party areas tend also to be more
homogeneous in population and political interests than competitive areas. Thus, the close linkage of electoral margin and representational role-taking is not an unexpected phenomenon.

Other evidence from our survey confirms this reasoning. Each
respondent was asked to react to a series of statements. One of
these was: "I seldom have to sound out my constituents because

I think so much like them that I know how to react to almost any proposal." Of the sample, 53 per cent indicated agreement with this statement. Trustees and Nationals, however, showed a greater disposition to agree with the proposition than Delegates or Locals, a fact that no doubt flows from the larger measure of freedom perceived by legislators from relatively safe districts. Another statement was: "As a Congressman I can do pretty much what I like here without worrying too much about criticism from my district." Trustees were in accord with the statement, 54 per cent to 38 per cent; of the Delegates, however, 30 per cent agreed and 70 per cent disagreed. Differences among respondents expressing various foci of representation were too slight to be significant, but nonetheless were in the anticipated direction.

Electoral risk affects representational roles similarly in all four regions—East, Midwest, South, and West.* In each region, members from safe districts are more apt to be Trustees or Nationals than those from marginal districts. The variations are especially acute in the East and West, and modest in the Midwest and South. Among southerners, however, both marginal and safe members are more Trustee-National oriented than the average member of the House. For example, in that region 53 per cent of the legislators from safe districts and 40 per cent from marginal districts indicated a national focus.

The impact of electoral risk is also felt in all types of districts—whether urban, rural, suburban, or some mixture of these.[41] In all cases competitive districts are associated with Delegate-Local roles and safe districts with Trustee-National roles. However, Congressmen from various types of districts do assume somewhat different styles of representation. Urban and rural members, for example, reflect significantly more Trustee-oriented roles than members from suburban or mixed districts. This difference does not appear to stem primarily from a concentration of safe or marginal districts in certain types of areas. Safe districts are somewhat over-represented in urban areas, a factor that may help explain the inclination of urban members toward the Trustee role. In other types of districts, however, the proportion of safe districts is fairly constant. Conceivably other factors are operative: the relative over-representation of leaders and Democrats in

*Regions are defined in the note on p. 44.

urban and rural areas, for example. Additionally, urban and rural districts may be objectively more homogenous than other types of districts, rendering the Representative's task somewhat more simple and giving him freedom to play the Trustee role. These remain speculations, because the numbers of respondents in our study are too small to permit analysis of the several relevant variables.

Because electoral risk is distributed unequally within the House, various subgroupings exhibit distinctive patterns of role-taking. Thus party affiliation, seniority, leadership status within the House, and other attributes are associated with the propensity of members to assume a distinctive style or focus of representation. Such attributes may in themselves exert an independent effect upon role-taking; but in large part the variations are attributable to differing levels of electoral risk among these subgroupings.

Prior speculation might suggest that party affiliation would have an impact upon representational roles. As indicated by Table 4–5, Republicans and Democrats do vary in their styles of representation. Republicans favor the Delegate end of the spectrum (33 per cent of the Republicans were Delegates, compared with 18 per cent of the Democrats), while Democrats were overwhelmingly Politicos (53 per cent) or even Trustees. These differences extend to every region, Democrats in each case tending toward the Trustee end of the scale and Republicans toward the Delegate role. The figures lend strength to the impression that Democrats are stylistically more oriented toward "playing the game" of balancing interests and constituencies than their Republican colleagues.[42]

Much of the difference between the two parties can be explained by variations among constituencies typically controlled by the two

Table 4–5. Party, Electoral Risk, and Representational Style

Role	Democrats			Republicans		
	Marginal	Safe	Total	Marginal	Safe	Total
Trustee	13%	36%	29%	24%	31%	27%
Politico	47	56	53	29	50	39
Delegate	40	8	18	47	19	33
Total	100%	100%	100%	100%	100%	99%
(n)	(15)	(36)	(51)	(17)	(16)	(33)
Style Index	1.73	2.28	2.11	1.77	2.12	1.92

parties. As a party, Republicans in the 88th Congress enjoyed fewer safe constituencies in the House than did the Democrats. More than half (51 per cent) of the Republicans in the sample came from marginal districts. The reverse was true of the Democrats, 70 per cent of whom came from safe districts.* Thus, when electoral risk is held constant, fewer interparty differences appear. Though marginal Democrats are more likely to be Politicos, in other respects they closely resemble marginal Republicans. Among Congressmen from less competitive districts, Democrats were somewhat more likely to be Trustees, though again they do not differ greatly from safe Republicans.

Similar partisan differences can be discerned in representational focus. (See Table 4-6.) A plurality of respondents in both parties, of course, were essentially Locals. But Democrats were twice as likely as Republicans to be Nationals, and were less likely to be Locals. Within each party, members from competitive districts tended to be Locals, while those from safe districts were more likely to be Nationals. Therefore, much of the partisan variation is traceable to the fact that Republicans as a group face greater electoral risks than their colleagues across the aisle. However, there is reason to suspect that party affiliation itself is influential. When competitiveness of district is held constant, Republicans in both categories are more district-oriented than their Democratic counterparts.

Table 4–6. Party, Electoral Risk, and Representational Focus

Role	Democrats			Republicans		
	Marginal	Safe	Total	Marginal	Safe	Total
National	25%	39%	35%	13%	24%	18%
Natl.-dist.	31	25	27	25	35	30
District	44	36	38	63	41	52
Total	100%	100%	100%	101%	100%	100%
(n)	(16)	(36)	(52)	(16)	(17)	(33)
Focal Index	1.81	2.14	1.97	1.52	1.83	1.66

*In the 88th Congress as a whole, 51 per cent of the Republicans and 35 per cent of the Democrats came from districts categorized here as marginal. Thus, the sample is very close to the distribution among the total universe. The large number of Republicans from marginal districts helps to explain the party's vulnerability to large Democratic shifts in the Presidential voting—and especially the party's large losses in the Johnson landslide of 1964.[43]

The pattern of Table 4-6 can be easily summarized: (a) Republicans from marginal districts are primarily Locals (63 per cent expressed a district focus); (b) safe Democrats are the most national grouping, with fully 39 per cent expressing primarily a National focus; (c) safe Republicans and marginal Democrats fall somewhere in the middle, and they manifest virtually identical patterns of role-taking.

While differences in electoral risk apparently fail to account for all of the party variation in representational roles, the actual explanation is not yet apparent. Political ideology itself does not seem to be the root of the variation: at least by one measure, the *Congressional Quarterly* "conservative coalition score," ideological voting patterns appear to bear no relation to representational roles. Two lines of explanation seem plausible, however. First, typical Republican districts may be more articulate and insistent in pressing claims before their elected representatives—quite apart from their level of competitiveness. We know that these districts are marked by relatively high educational attainment, large proportions of white-collar and professional workers, and high average rankings on other measures of achieved status.[44] These attributes are typically associated with political activism, and it is not unreasonable to suppose that districts which rank higher in such attributes are more vocal in communicating their wishes to their Congressmen. Insofar as his constituents exhibit information about, and involvement in, political issues, the legislator may find he can ill afford to play Trustee or National roles.

A second possible explanation lies in divergent patterns of socialization in the House. Perhaps, for example, newer members are inducted into different styles of operation related to the different responsibilities of the majority and minority party. The unique demands of majority-party leadership may thus draw Democratic members more frequently into the ranks of the House Nationals. Obviously the present data cannot give verification to this hypothesis.

The findings thus far may be summarized as follows: First, in both parties electorally marginal districts are associated with Delegate and Local roles; safe districts, by contrast, are associated with Trustee and National roles. Second, Republicans are more apt to express Delegate and Local roles, while Democrats are more attracted to Trustee and National roles. This phenomenon is certainly related to the comparative insulation of House Democrats from electoral risk: In the sample and in the House as a whole, a large majority of Democrats had the good fortune to represent relatively safe constituencies. Republican members, by contrast, were about evenly divided between safe and competitive districts. However, partisan variations in representational focus (and style, to a degree) are also related to other (as yet undetermined) factors—perhaps variations in constituency characteristics or intra-House socialization.

Aside from party affiliation, one of the most important attributes of members in the House is unquestionably the amount of seniority they possess. High seniority not only implies that the member has a firm electoral base at home; it serves on Capitol Hill as a key to the doors of influence and formal leadership. The relation of seniority to representational roles can be easily inferred from our discussion thus far, and in general the findings—as revealed in Table 4–7—bear out our expectations. That is, Trustee and National roles are related positively to length of service in the House of Representatives. Average index scores rise with seniority (especially for middle-seniority members), indicating a movement toward Trustee and National orientations.

The seniority groupings were arranged to permit analysis of the perspectives of newcomers to Congress—the "freshman class." Although the number of freshmen is considerably smaller than in the remaining groups, these members clearly find the Delegate style most attractive. A clear majority (56 per cent) of the first-termers in our sample were Delegates; only 13 per cent manifested Trustee orientations. Of the high-seniority respondents (those with six or more terms of service) 38 per cent were Trustees, and only 18 per cent were Delegates. Middle-seniority members (two to five terms) tended to resemble their more senior colleagues. Large numbers of Politicos were found at all seniority levels, though the role was somewhat more prevalent among middle- and high-seniority members.

Seniority relates directly also to focus of representation, although here the differences are less striking and exist mainly between freshmen members and all others. Exactly half of the first-termers exhibited primarily a district focus, compared with 42 per cent in the middle- and high-seniority groups. And while only 12 per cent of the freshmen were Nationals, the figures for middle- and

Table 4–7. Seniority and Representational Roles Among 87 Members of the House

Style	Members, by Number of Terms Seniority			Focus	Members, by Number of Terms Seniority		
	One	2 to 5	6–plus		One	2 to 5	6–plus
Trustee	13%	26%	38%	National	12%	33%	30%
Politico	31	59	44	Natl.-dist.	38·	24	27
Delegate	56	15	18	District	50	42	42
Total	100%	100%	100%	Total	100%	100%	99%
(n)	(16)	(34)	(34)	(n)	(16)	(36)	(33)
Style Index	1.57	2.11	2.20	Focal Index	1.62	1.92	1.86

high-seniority respondents were 33 per cent and 30 per cent respectively. Particularly among freshmen Congressmen, the percentage of respondents expressing each of the constituency foci parallels closely the distribution among the corresponding styles. However, among members with higher seniority the Local focus remains strong, while the Delegate style is relatively rare among members above the freshman term.

Table 4–8. Party, Leadership, and Representational Style Among 113 Members of the House[a]

Style	Leaders			Nonleaders		
	Democrat	Republican	Total	Democrat	Republican	Total
Trustee	38%	24%	31%	26%	29%	27%
Politico	48	71	60	56	32	46
Delegate	14	5	10	19	39	27
Total	101%	100%	101%	101%	100%	100%
(n)	(21)	(21)	(42)	(43)	(28)	(71)
Style Index	2.24	2.19	2.23	2.06	1.90	2.00

a Because of the few leaders in the general sample of 87 members, we have added respondents in the leadership over-samples when comparing leadership status with other variables. This produces some slight discrepancies in the average index scores, since these scores are slightly higher for the augmented sample than for the general sample. For a definition of the leadership over-samples, see note, p. 77.

Similarly predictable patterns emerge when leadership status is examined, as in Tables 4–8 and 4–9. House leaders are somewhat more likely than nonleaders to exhibit Trustee and National roles; and they are considerably less likely to be Delegates or Locals. What might be termed the compromise roles—Politico and National-Local—are particularly prevalent among leaders. In each instance, too, the partisan variable appears to carry some weight.

That is, irrespective of formal leadership status, Democrats in all categories tend somewhat toward the Trustee-National end of the spectrum, while Republicans are inclined toward Delegate-Local roles.

As a general proposition, the level of electoral risk—as indicated by margin of victory in the preceding election—is responsible for differences in role-taking between low-seniority and high-seniority members, and between nonleaders and leaders. Indeed, the three variables are closely intertwined. Freshmen members come disproportionately from competitive areas, while higher seniority members tend to come from safe districts. Similarly, leaders are likely to represent safe constituencies. Needless to add, leadership position in the House is also a function of length of service: All the leaders in the present sample, for example, possessed at least six terms of seniority.

Table 4–9. Party, Leadership, and Representational Focus Among 114 Members of the House[a]

| | Leaders | | | Nonleaders | | |
Focus	Democrat	Republican	Total	Democrat	Republican	Total
National	33%	38%	36%	32%	21%	28%
Natl.-dist.	52	38	45	25	29	26
District	14	24	19	43	50	46
Total	99%	100%	100%	100%	100%	100%
(n)	(21)	(21)	(42)	(44)	(28)	(72)
Focal Index	2.18	2.14	2.17	1.89	1.74	1.82

a Includes leader over-samples.

The congruence of these variables, however, poses an acute problem of analysis. Seniority, leadership position, and electoral risk are all related to members' representational role cognitions. But to what extent is the relationship of each variable independent of the others? Does the hypothetical newcomer to Capitol Hill assume a Delegate orientation because he is a newcomer, because he has gained election by a narrow margin, or because he lacks leadership responsibilities? Conversely, why does a House leader —a committee chairman or a party whip, for example—focus his attentions on the national constituency? Is it his leadership responsibilities, or his relative lack of qualms over re-election, or his accumulated experience in the House? Such queries are hardly novel to students of legislative behavior.

The present sample lacks a sufficient number of cases to permit confident answers to such questions as these. By pushing the data to their limits (and perhaps beyond), however, a few tentative conclusions can be ventured.

Seniority probably works independently to stimulate the Trustee style of representation. To be sure, a large part of the effect stems from the fact that less experienced legislators are more likely to represent competitive districts (only three freshmen interviewees represented *safe* districts, while only three of the most senior—six terms or more—members came from *marginal* districts). At all seniority levels Congressmen from safe districts are more Trustee-oriented than those from unsafe districts. However, the few freshmen from safe districts were as Trustee-prone as their senior colleagues from safe districts. Freshmen from marginal districts, however, were by far the most Delegate-oriented grouping in the House (69 per cent were Delegates).

Thus, degree of electoral competition may be more salient to inexperienced members than to others. Senior legislators are less moved by their margin of victory; having survived the vicissitudes of re-election campaigning, they are able to assess their position with somewhat more confidence. Our definition of safe and marginal districts, too, is less meaningful at the upper seniority levels: Incumbents who win consistently, even though by relatively modest margins, may in fact represent safe districts.

The separate impact of leadership status upon representational style is more doubtful. Although leaders are strongly inclined to express Trustee or Politico roles, they exhibit other attributes associated with these roles: They possess considerable seniority and are overwhelmingly from safe districts. Thus, when electoral risk is held constant, leaders seem no more Trustee-oriented than high-seniority Congressmen who are not leaders.

A slightly different pattern emerges for focus of representation. On the one hand, the data suggest that seniority itself has no bearing on the likelihood that members will assume National rather than Local roles. The relatively National orientation of senior Congressmen seems almost entirely a function of the relative electoral safety they enjoy.

On the other hand, leadership position does appear to exert an independent push in the direction of a National orientation. Leaders are thus more National in focus than nonleaders of similar seniority and electoral safety. High-seniority nonleaders, in contrast, are no more inclined to a National focus than nonleaders in general. As a result, these high-seniority nonleaders tend to assume a Local orientation (resembling lower-seniority nonleaders) but a Trustee style (resembling leaders).

A final question concerns the relationship of representational roles to the legislator's purposive definitions of their jobs. In Chapter 3 we presented two measures of purposive orientation: first, the so-called purposive role (a phenomenon first identified by Wahlke and his colleagues); and second, a crude indicator of the members' time-allocations, which we termed "focus of activity." In many instances the two measures coincided; but they also differ, insofar as the legislators' normative job-descriptions may diverge from their actual day-to-day activities.

We would expect purposive and representational roles to be related. After all, some of the factors associated with purposive role are also associated with representational style or focus. Perhaps, too, purposive role itself serves as an independent variable. Whatever the precise paths of causality, the relationships may be seen in Tables 4–10 and 4–11.

Table 4–10. Purposive Role and Representational Styles of 84 Members of the House

| | Purposive Role | | | | |
Style	Tribune	Ritualist	Inventor	Broker	Opportunist
Trustee	10%	47%	67%		
Politico	50	44	33	100%	
Delegate	40	9			100%
Total	100%	100%	100%	100%	100%
(n)	(40)	(34)	(6)	(3)	(1)
Style Index	1.70	2.38	2.67	2.00	1.00

Table 4–11. Purposive Role and Representational Foci of 85 Members of the House

| | Purposive Role | | | | |
Focus	Tribune	Ritualist	Inventor	Broker	Opportunist
National	12%	50%	83%	33%	
Natl.-dist.	24	24	17	33	
District	63	27		33	100%
Total	99%	101%	100%	99%	100%
(n)	(41)	(34)	(6)	(3)	(1)
Focal Index	1.47	2.25	2.83	2.00	1.00

As we observed in the previous chapter, Tribunes and Ritualists were the only categories that appeared in sufficient strength to permit meaningful generalizations. These two roles, it will be recalled, reflect widespread norms concerning the meaning of legislative office—the Tribune embracing the ideal of representing external constituencies, and the Ritualist emphasizing tasks internal to the legislative body. Though both themes command broad support among our sample, they receive somewhat varying emphasis among our respondents; and we have tried to capture these variations by using primary purposive roles for analysis. From what we learned about these purposive orientations, we would expect Tribunes to emphasize constituency-centered notions of representation, while Ritualists would be expected to turn their attention away from their constituencies. Tables 4–10 and 4–11 indicate that this is indeed the case. Tribunes are overwhelmingly Delegate-Politicos and Locals. In contrast, Ritualists are drawn toward Trustee and National roles.

Other purposive orientations appear in small numbers, but it is instructive to note that in every case they turn up in the predicted cells. Inventors are among the most Trustee- and National-oriented members in the House. Brokers are also Politicos who exhibit varying foci of representation. The lone Opportunist, of course, is a Delegate and a Local.

The legislator's focus of activity is also related to his style and focus of representation. Trustees and Nationals tend to devote more emphasis to legislative responsibilities than other members of the House—though these tasks were strongly emphasized by all respondents. Of the Trustees and Nationals in our sample, 88 per cent focused upon legislative tasks and 13 per cent on Errand Boy and other constituency tasks (the percentages were identical). Among Delegates and Locals, however, there was a somewhat greater disposition to engage in constituency work. Only 65 per cent of the Delegates and 68 per cent of the Locals were legislators, while 35 per cent and 32 per cent (respectively) were Errand Boys or Mentor-Communicators.

Finally, it is relevant to note that—as with purposive role—social background variables offer very little explanation for the member's choice of representational style or focus. Thus, there is no significant relationship between occupation and representational role. Nor is there a relationship between level of educational attainment and these roles. (Educational differences, however, are not great among our respondents: Only 20 per cent possess less than a college degree, for example.) Nor does there seem to be a significant relationship between political experience and representational style or focus. Here again, discrepancies among respondents are minimal, since all but 6 per cent had discernible political experience prior to election to the House. But such discrepancies as exist offer little help to the analyst: State legislators, for example, display no different approaches to representation than members who lack such experience.

CONCLUSIONS: LOCAL YOKELS AND STATESMEN

How the member of Congress chooses to respond to constituents' claims is one of the truly large questions with which students of politics must deal. Democratic political theory, voters' expectations, and political scientists' curiosity about "influence and the influential" all conspire to render the member's representational role of critical importance both to himself and others. In this chapter we have approached two central questions about the Congressman-as-representative: Is the Congressman listening? If so, to whom?

In answer to these questions, it has been found that Congressmen vary considerably in style and focus of representation. Some members assume the role of the Trustee, relying upon their own information or conscience in making up their minds. Others are Delegates, who prefer to consult constituents' wishes (or their own understanding of those wishes) in making decisions. Still others—about half of the present sample—play the Politico role, combining their opinions with those of constituents, acting upon one or the other or both as the situation dictates. While Congressmen are not mindless slaves to outside pressures, they nonetheless do not think themselves as free as some students have suggested.

What constituencies are listened to also varies greatly among members. Some are attuned primarily to the national constituency, others to their electorate back home, still others to both of these. And while members of the House are more local (or parochial) than their critics would like them to be, a large number are acutely aware of their responsibility for the welfare of people whose needs or interests diverge from those of their electorate.

Most would probably concur with the member who appealed to his colleagues to vote for a bill needed in his urban district. Reminding the membership that they had legislated on behalf of many specialized interests, he explained that new expenditures were needed to forestall racial violence in his city.

> Every member of Congress [he concluded] faces difficult problems which result from our varied constituencies. We are here in the common purpose of solving the problem of every other constituency in America. We take the same oath. We share the same obligations wherever we live.[45]

Unlike purposive role orientation, style and focus of representation are largely extensions of the member's electoral safety or vulnerability. As the Congressman assesses the extent of trouble he is likely to face at the polls, so he tends to perceive the claims that others make on his behavior. If he expects potent opposition in the next campaign, he is very likely to be a Delegate whose focus is on his district. If he is more fortunate and has a relatively safe seat, he can afford to select the Trustee role or National focus. This fact alone produces distinctive representational orientations among various categories of members. Trustee and National roles are more common among Democrats, leaders, southerners, and high-seniority members. Delegate and Local roles are more typical of Republicans, nonleaders, nonsoutherners, and freshmen.

Although electoral facts of life account for most of the differences in Representatives' style and focus, other factors appear to exercise some independent influence. The propensity of Republicans to assume Delegate or Local roles, for example, is probably related to distinctive attributes of Republican districts, or to divergent patterns of intra-House socialization. In addition, high seniority seems to exert an independent push in the direction of the Trustee style, while leadership is associated with a National focus.

The impact of electoral vulnerability upon the legislator's freedom to maneuver is commonly accepted by both the mythology and science of American politics. Politicians clearly understand the pathos of the story told of one recent House member, a California Democrat. As a liberal, he had looked forward to the decennial redistricting in 1961 by the Democratic-controlled state legislature. He hoped that his competitive district could be redrawn so that liberal voters would safely outnumber conservatives. The legislature, though it lost few chances to shape the state's Congressional districts in accord with partisan interests, happened to leave this man's district untouched. "I could have been a statesman if they had cut off a few of those conservatives," the member lamented. "Now I'll have to continue going this way and that way, back and forth. I'm a cracker-ass Congressman—and I could have been a statesman!" The poor fellow's plight would no doubt be echoed by many of his colleagues. A recent empirical study, an audit of incoming communications cues for six Congressmen, has found that the member's receptivity to cues varied positively with his vulnerability at the polls.[46]

Although this understanding is hardly contested by most students of politics, its implications are too often unappreciated. Positive values are usually attached both to political competition and to statesmanlike courage or the national point of view; one-party districts (often preceded by the adjective "stagnant") and parochial Congressmen are usually valued negatively. The present author does not wish to dissent from these valuations. But it should be remembered that these attributes do not necessarily go together; indeed, they may be incompatible under normal circumstances. Whatever the benefits of electoral competition, it does not tend to produce Congressmen who are Trustees or who are free to take a national view of things. And whatever the vices of safe districts, they *do* tend to produce just such members. This is not to say, of course, that Delegates-Locals are venal or that Trustees-Nationals are custodians of the public interest. It is merely to re-emphasize that a legislator's freedom of action may be purchased at the price of electoral competition.*

Leaving aside the possible policy biases of one-partyism (and these may be very important indeed), it would appear that a very significant *institutional* function is served by the presence of members from both types of districts. On the one hand, our political framework requires that legislators, or at least a good portion of them, possess the kind of enforced sensitivity to public attitudes

---

*Of course, many who criticize Congressmen who happen to come disproportionately from one-party areas—e.g., the archetypical southern conservative or the northern organization politician—do so for policy reasons. But this argument has little to do with the scope of the member's freedom; rather, it is a complaint that the members in question are not subjected to the kinds of localized pressures with which the critics are in agreement.

that electoral competition produces. On the other hand, the House is a large and complex institution, requiring the labors of members whose electoral good fortune allows them to tend to its business. The committee leaders, policy experts, and political entrepreneurs of the House are unquestionably aided, and their time budgets made more manageable, by the fact that many of them have only minimal pressures from the folks back home. In fact, the complicated division of labor that has evolved in the House would most likely be impossible if all the districts were poised at the electoral tipping-point. From a functional point of view, then, Trustees and Delegates, Nationals and Locals, all make important contributions to the life of our national legislature.

CHAPTER 5

PARTY AND
INTEREST-GROUP ROLES

Thus far we have examined several classes of attributes that help to define the place members of Congress occupy in our political scheme of things. Initially, we considered two closely related sets of variables that provide a generalized answer to the question, "Who is the Congressman?" These variables were associated with social background and the political career. While no direct relationship can be inferred between these attributes and the roles Congressmen assume once in office, it can be argued that such factors have an important bearing on legislative role-taking. The way roles are articulated and the degree of congruence among roles, for example, may well be a function of homogeneity among the members of Congress. Similar social or occupational backgrounds, as well as shared experiences as political apprentices, must be understood if we are to fathom the behavior of Congressmen.

The Representative's perspectives on his legislative tasks, as evidenced by our interviews with a sample of members in the 88th Congress, have also been described in some detail. The purposive role, or sense of the ultimate aim of legislative activities, was employed to measure the member's over-all conception of his job. Two dimensions of the representational role—style and focus—were also described at length. Though somewhat more limited in scope than the purposive role, these representational orientations influence the legislator's responses to a wide range of demands made upon him.

Other roles are relevant in charting the dimensions of the legislator's job. Orientations toward committee work or the procedural aspects of House routine, for example, will influence his allocation of time and energy, his relationships with fellow members, even his effectiveness in bargaining. His role vis-à-vis the President or the executive apparatus is, especially in this age of executive ascendancy, a critical determinant of his activities on Capitol Hill. His role in local party organizations, or in voluntary associations, may be equally important. In addition, some roles that the member holds in common with private citizens—as member of a family or of an informal social grouping, for instance—may upon occasion impinge upon his legislative tasks. Clearly, a comprehensive view of *the* role of the legislator must embrace his orientations toward all those things in his environment that affect or condition his behavior on Capitol Hill.[1] Unfortunately, not all of these role orientations are equally accessible to the student of legislative behavior.

Two specific role dimensions, however, touch upon aspects of the legislative environment that all observers identify as especially important. These are the member's responses to his political party and to private groups making claims upon the legislature. One of the most important facts about an elected official is his membership in a political party. State or district party organizations usually promote or sponsor his career; his national party provides a label, which he may encourage or shun; and party leaders within the House cajole his votes and call upon his loyalty. Interest groups, though primarily outside the legislature, are attributed importance by nearly all observers because they supply the members with information, and sometimes pressure, on particular issues. At minimum, such groups serve as positive or negative references for legislators, who can gauge their own position by taking readings of the groups' positions. In the present chapter we attempt to describe the members' orientations toward party and interest groups, using data from our 1963–1964 survey of the House of Representatives.

The roles described here should be interpreted as generalized attitudes toward objects in the legislator's environment.* As such,

---

*The "roles" discussed in this chapter are somewhat different from the role prescriptions analyzed thus far. The difference is more methodological than analytical. In the case of purposive and representational roles, the respondents' attitudes were indicated in open-

they will not be related here to specific behaviors. The central purpose of this inquiry, as we have stressed previously, is to describe the kinds of roles articulated by members, the distribution of these roles within the House, and some of the factors associated with role-taking.

Table 5–1. Attitudes of 87 Congressmen Toward Political Parties[a]

Item	Agree	Tend to Agree	Undecided	Tend to Disagree	Disagree	No Answer
The best interests of the people would be better served if Congressmen were elected without party labels.	7%	3%	3%	14%	70%	2%
Under our form of government, every individual should take an interest in government directly, not through a political party.	17%	12%	5%	20%	46%	1%
If a bill is important for his party's record, a member should vote with his party even if it costs him some support in his district.	9%	26%	7%	15%	37%	6%
The two parties should take clear-cut, opposing stands on more of the important and controversial issues.	17%	28%	3%	16%	35%	1%

a These items are adapted from John C. Wahlke et al., The Legislative System (New York: John Wiley, 1962), pp. 502–503.

ended responses to the query, "What should you do as a Congressman?" Party and interest-group roles, by contrast, were extrapolated from responses to forced-answer items in the questionnaire. It might be argued that the element of self-prescription is weaker in the latter form of question. Whether or not this is the case, we are justified in inferring role cognitions from the respondents' answers. The legislator's generalized assessment of an object in his environment—his party organization, for example—implies a self-prescribed stance toward the object. It is in this inferential sense that we will refer to partisan- and interest-group-attitude dimensions as roles.

PARTISAN ROLES: LOYALISTS AND MAVERICKS

The Congressional parties, like political parties generally, are the despair of friends and critics alike. As unifying forces, they must strive mightily against the decentralizing tendencies inherent in the legislative situation: the pull of constituency interests and the semiautonomy of the committee structure. Linkages between the Congressional parties and the national parties, too, are oftentimes tenuous. When a legislative party is subject to leadership from the White House, the relationship can be described at best as "functional interdependence";[2] when the party does not control the Presidency, the bonds may be even less taut. Nor do the parties always differentiate themselves clearly on policy issues: As V. O. Key, Jr., remarked, "partisan differences must be described in terms of modalities, not dichotomies."[3] Looking with horror at the seeming chaos of the party organizations, not a few observers have urged that steps be taken to achieve a modicum of "party government" within the houses of Congress.[4]

On the other hand, the political parties remain the most stable and important groupings in Congress. Though party discipline is imperfect, party identification is strong; and party affiliation is the strongest correlate of voting behavior in the two houses.[5] In large measure, this party unity rests upon similarities of district characteristics and, inferentially, similarities of attitudes and interests. Thus, Republican Congressmen, for example, tend to take similar positions on issues because they come from districts with "Republican" characteristics, such as high income, lower urbanization, high percentage of owner-occupied dwellings, and low proportion of nonwhite residents.[6] By the same token, Republicans stray from the party fold when their constituencies deviate from the party norm in some way crucial to the issue at hand.

While this explanation accounts for basic characteristics of party voting, it tends to overstate the magnitude of constituency demands. As we discovered in Chapter 4, Congressmen hold varying conceptions of the place of constituency in their decision-making.[7] These conceptions roughly reflect the salience of constituency demands as evidenced by the threat of defeat at the polls. Given these differences in constituency pressures, party leaders have numerous opportunities to serve as cue-givers for their rank-and-file. Nor should the reality of the legislative parties as organizations be ignored. Congressmen tend to form friendships within party lines, and psychological pressures tend to push members toward agreement with the majority in their party. Moreover, party chieftains can have an impact in persuading members to support the party's positions on issues.[8] For these and other reasons, party affiliation constitutes the single most important group loyalty for members of Congress.

One measure of the orientations of members toward their political parties lies in their generalized attitudes concerning the importance of parties, the legitimacy of party activity, and the priority that individual legislators should give to party positions. In the present study these attitudes were indicated by responses to four closed-ended questions from our survey of members of the 88th Congress. Three of these questions form a scale from which partisan role dispositions can be extracted. Responses to the four questions are presented in Table 5-1.

Widespread acceptance of the legitimacy of political parties was evidenced in answers to the more modest party-oriented propositions. No more than 10 per cent of the respondents supported the idea that Congressmen should be elected without party labels. (One Republican leader with long service wryly observed that though he could probably win the Democratic primary in his district, it would not serve the public's need to have opposing candidates put up.) Only 29 per cent thought that citizens should try to influence their government directly, without recourse to political parties. Interviewee comments suggested that those who agreed with the statement were casting a vote for individual citizen involvement rather than against partisan involvement.

When more demanding tests of party loyalty are used, however, opinions are more evenly divided. Slightly more than a third of the respondents believed they should support their party at the cost of some support in the district. But an equal number strongly opposed this notion. Party loyalty, it seems, must contend with strong opposing forces. Ripley found, for example, that Congressmen of both parties felt a strong desire to go along with their party; but virtually all the members he interviewed mentioned constituency and conscience as reasons for opposing party demands.[9] Such reasons are considered legitimate even by party leaders, as evidenced by the following comments of our interviewees:

> [Should a Congressman vote for his party against his constitu-
> ents?] . . . It depends on the known will of the constituents. The
> Representative must realize he's a true servant of the people—he
> should do for them what they would do for themselves if they
> had a vote. Besides, no party expects 100 per cent support. [South-
> ern Democratic leader, rural district]

> [As the respondent indicated strong disagreement with the state-
> ment:] I'm a party whip and I don't like the question. [Southern
> Democratic leader, mixed district]

Yet party leaders do exercise influence in marshaling votes, and
some members are resentful of this:

> My most pressing problem is balancing between my votes on
> one side, and the Congress on the other—especially the Estab-
> lishment, the pyramidal, formal leadership headed by the Speaker.
> [Respondent contrasted a recent vote on the farm bill, which
> "pleased the Leadership as well as my constituents," with a con-
> templated vote on the depressed areas bill which "will be pro-
> leadership but won't benefit my constituents."] Fear of reprisals,
> especially water projects for my area, is very great. [Southern
> Democratic nonleader, rural district]

Psychological pressures also induce legislators to go along with
their party. When they are unable to co-operate, many feel frustrations which are very real. As one discouraged Southerner
remarked,

> My philosophy isn't as liberal as the President's—or as liberal
> as many of my supporters. But I don't like to take positions that
> I don't believe in—yet I am a Democrat and that is important to
> me. I just have to try to avoid the things that I don't go along with.
> [Southern Democratic nonleader, rural district]

Clearly the claims of party loyalty represent strong influences upon
Congressmen; but opposing demands create tensions in making
decisions.

Forty-five per cent of the interviewees felt the parties should
take more clear-cut stands on the issues. Here again, though, more
than a third expressed strong disagreement. And again constituency and conscience were cited as reasons for minimizing party
issues.

> Each bill should be approached individually. Too many mem-
> bers vote on ideology, without thinking through each bill. And
> there are too many partisan political issues in the House. Some-
> times party-line votes are hasty majorities. [Western Republican
> nonleader, urban district]

The picture that emerges from these responses is one of over-whelming support for the norm of party activity but considerable disagreement over the degree of loyalty that party membership should imply.

In order to examine the factors accompanying these partisan attitudes, we have taken three of the four response items and ranked respondents by the extent to which their answers were proparty.* Combining each respondent's answers to the three items, we are able to divide the Congressmen into four groupings: Superloyalists, Loyalists, Neutrals, and Mavericks.† Although the boundaries between categories are necessarily somewhat arbitrary, we can consider the categories as rough indicators of members' over-all disposition toward their political party and the level of demands it can legitimately make upon them. Hence, we refer to these attitudinal categories as roles, even though they are derived differently than the roles described in previous chapters.

The distribution of partisan roles among the eighty-six mem-bers whose responses were classifiable is shown in Table 5-2. If an index is constructed from the continuum of party loyalty repre-sented by the four role types, the average party index score for the entire sample is 2.61 (on a scale of 4.0).‡ On the dimension of partisan loyalty, then, the center of gravity for our respondents can be identified as falling between the Loyalist and Neutralist roles, and slightly closer to the former than to the latter. This finding is consistent with the generally held view of Congressional parties as important but nonetheless loose alliances.

Republicans as a group have a slightly higher average party index than their Democratic colleagues. Confirmation for this modest variance is found by comparing party roles with the party unity scores compiled by *Congressional Quarterly*. In the 88th

*The "party government" item (the last item of Table 5-1) was omitted from the analysis because it appeared to tap a slightly different attitude dimension.

†Each proposition permitted five gradations of response: agree (with proparty position), tend to agree, undecided, tend to disagree, and disagree. (For two of the items, of course, the proparty responses were negative.) Responses to each item were weighted from 1 to 5, cumulated, and averaged for each respondent. Therefore, a perfect proparty score would be 5.0; a perfect antiparty score 1.0. From the respondents' scores, four categories were drawn: Superloyalists (scoring between 4.7 and 5.0); Loyalists (3.7 through 4.3); Neutrals (2.5 through 3.3); and Mavericks (1.0 through 2.3).

‡ A simple index score was assigned to each respondent on the following basis: Super-loyalist, 4; Loyalist, 3; Neutral, 2; Maverick, 1. Index scores were then averaged for the population in question—in this case, the total sample of 86.

Table 5–2. Party Roles Among 86 Congressmen

Superloyalist	23%
Loyalist	37
Neutral	21
Maverick	19
Total	100%
(n)	(86)
Party Index	2.64

Table 5–3. Party Affiliation and Party Roles Among 86 Congressmen

Role	Democrats	Republicans
Superloyalist	17%	29%
Loyalist	42	29
Neutral	19	24
Maverick	21	18
Total	99%	100%
(n)	(52)	(34)
Party Index	2.53	2.69

Congress, House Republicans on the average supported their party in 72 per cent of the party votes, while Democrats upheld their party in 71 per cent of the votes.* In other Congressional sessions during the early and mid-1960's, Republicans have shown an even greater disposition toward party unity, in comparison with their Democratic colleagues, than in the 88th Congress. In no case does the evidence suggest great variation between the parties; but it would seem that the Republicans have been slightly more cohesive than Democrats—at least during the years in question.†

*The party unity score, devised by *Congressional Quarterly,* represents the percentage of times the member votes with his party on "party votes" (*i.e.,* votes in which a majority of one party opposes a majority of the other party).[10] We have recomputed party unity scores for each of our respondents by dividing the percentage of times each supported his party in the 88th Congress by the sum of his party unity percentage and his party opposition percentage. This procedure removes the effect of absences during roll-call votes. Among Democratic respondents, average party unity scores were as follows: Superloyalists, 96; Loyalists, 90; Neutrals, 69; Mavericks, 68. Among Republicans, the scores were: Superloyalists, 81; Loyalists, 89; Neutrals, 80; Mavericks, 77.

†If correct, this conclusion casts some doubt upon David B. Truman's hypothesis that a "Presidential" majority party in Congress should display greater cohesion than a "truncated" majority.[11] The transformation of Congressional Democrats from a "truncated" to a "Presidential" majority in the 1960 election apparently was not accompanied by an over-all rise in party cohesion, if party unity scores are used as the measure. In the field of foreign policy, however, Truman's hypothesis does seem to be valid.[12]

Leaders tend to be slightly more party-oriented than nonleaders, a finding reflected in Table 5–4. Fully 20 per cent of those without formal leadership position can be classed as Mavericks, while only half that proportion of leaders can be so classed. On the other hand, leaders are slightly more apt to take Superloyalist or Loyalist roles. When party and leadership status are compared, as in Table 5–5, the two variables can be observed. In both parties, leaders are more apt to assume Loyalist roles than are nonleaders. Moreover, in both groupings Republicans tend to be more party-oriented than their Democratic counterparts—with Republican leaders evidencing the highest party orientation and Democratic followers the lowest. Republican followers and Democratic leaders fall in the middle, each group scoring an identical average party index. The level of party loyalty expressed by leaders is actually more impressive than it appears in these tables; for, as we see presently, Congressional leaders are drawn from groups in the House that normally display the lowest party orientation.

Table 5–4. Leadership and Party Roles Among 114 Congressmen[a]

Role	Leaders	Nonleaders
Superloyalist	23%	22%
Loyalist	45	38
Neutral	23	20
Maverick	10	20
Total	101%	100%
(n)	(40)	(74)
Party Index	2.83	2.62

a Figures include leader over-sample. (See note, p. 000.)

Table 5–5. Party Affiliation, Leadership Status, and Party Roles Among 114 Congressmen

Role	Democrats		Republicans	
	Leaders	Nonleaders	Leaders	Nonleaders
Superloyalist	11%	18%	33%	28%
Loyalist	63	40	29	35
Neutral	16	20	29	21
Maverick	11	22	10	17
Total	101%	100%	101%	101%
(n)	(19)	(45)	(21)	(29)
Party Index	2.76	2.54	2.87	2.76

Our findings thus far might imply that party role is positively correlated with seniority—a factor closely associated with leadership status in the House. This further assumption is not borne out, as the figures in Table 5-6 demonstrate. In fact, the tendency seems to be exactly the reverse. Party-centered roles predominate among first-termers, none of whom could be classified as a Maverick. Among Congressmen with some degree of seniority, however, the ratio of Superloyalists and Loyalists declines. And members with six or more terms of service seem least inclined to display Loyalist orientations toward their political parties. Indeed, one third of those in this category could be classed as Mavericks, while less than half that number are Superloyalists. The center of gravity for each of the three groups—represented by the party index averages—declines steadily with rising seniority, with the freshman group falling squarely on the Loyalist role and the high-seniority group closer to the Neutral role. From his analysis of party voting in the same Congress, Ripley also concluded that, in general, seniority is related negatively to party loyalty.[13]

Table 5–6. Seniority and Party Role Among 86 Congressmen

| Role | Members, by Seniority | | |
	One Term	2–5 Terms	6–Plus Terms
Superloyalist	29%	25%	15%
Loyalist	41	39	33
Neutral	29	19	18
Maverick		17	33
Total	99%	100%	101%
(n)	(17)	(36)	(33)
Party Index	2.97	2.72	2.28

The propensity of first-term Congressmen to assume party Loyalist roles is not difficult to understand. From the moment he arrives in Washington (and perhaps before), the freshman Congressman is reminded repeatedly of the role his party leadership can play in advancing his career. Irwin N. Gertzog, in his study of Republican freshmen of the 89th Congress, has noted that the influences upon newcomers are primarily party-based.[14] One of the newly elected legislator's first chores is to pay calls upon his party's leaders and ranking members on the standing committees, as well as colleagues in his own delegation and other freshmen of his own party. Particularly significant in embellishing his career is a suitable committee assignment—a decision that rests with his party leadership, members of his party's committee on committees, the dean of his state's delegation, and influential members of the committees in question.[15] The first-termer also relies on many of these same people to help him learn the ropes—to provide advice on selecting a staff, finding a place to live in the nation's capital, establishing an office regimen, establishing rapport with his constituents, and a hundred other problems both large and small.

Party identification is reinforced by party organizations, both formal and informal. (In the Republican party, each incoming "class" has a formally organized club, which meets regularly and helps to socialize members into the Capitol Hill environment.) In the committee rooms and on the floor, the newcomer tends to turn to others of his own party for advice, information, and voting cues. As a result, freshmen often have impressive records of voting with their party.[16] In short, "in these early days, [the newcomer's] political party [is] the great organizing factor in his private and public life."[17] Inexperienced, concerned over re-election, representing a district which is likely to be politically competitive, dependent upon party leadership for crucial boosts to his career, the freshman Congressman seeks protection in close identification with his party.

The lower incidence of party-centered roles among high-seniority members is more difficult to explain. Of course, the very forces that propel the newcomer into the bosom of the party organization may seem less compelling to the veteran legislator. With one or more re-election campaigns under his belt, he can view his career with somewhat more confidence. He has developed his own style of maintaining rapport with his constituents—sometimes by carving out a position distinct from that of his national party. His independence is encouraged by the fact that he is more likely than his freshman colleagues to represent a safe district. Within the House of Representatives, the veteran Congressman is less apt to need the services provided by the party organization: His committee assignment is usually fixed, and he has developed a network of informal communications with House colleagues who can supply him with the information he needs. On the other hand, growing seniority brings with it the possibility of a leadership post; and we have already seen that leaders are somewhat more inclined to be loyal party men. Is it not reasonable, then, to associate seniority with leadership status, and hence with party-oriented roles?

The answer is that seniority and leadership appear to bear very different relationships to party role. This can be demonstrated by examining the party roles of high-seniority leaders and nonleaders. Partisan roles of leaders were presented in the first and third columns of Table 5–5 (it will be recalled that all leaders had six or more terms of service). The number of nonleader respondents with six or more terms is relatively small, but the data clearly indicate that they are not, by and large, party men. In fact, half of the Republicans and 41 per cent of the Democrats in this category are classed as Mavericks. The difference between these Congressmen and formal leaders with similar seniority can be discerned by inspection of Table 5–5 and by comparison of the party index scores of the two groups. These scores are summarized in Table 5–7.

Table 5–7. Average Party Index Scores of High-Seniority Members

Democratic leaders	2.76
Republican leaders	2.87
All leaders	2.83
Democratic nonleaders	2.06
Republican nonleaders	2.25
All nonleaders	2.10

It seems clear that high-seniority leaders and nonleaders tend to adopt quite different party roles. Leadership is associated with Loyalist roles, while lack of leadership status is associated with Neutral and Maverick roles. The divergence is particularly impressive when it is recalled that the leadership category includes not only party leaders but committee chairmen and ranking minority members as well. There are only six party leaders in the sample (Speaker, two floor leaders, two chief whips, and the Republican Conference Chairman): All are Loyalists except one, who is a Neutral. By contrast, a few committee leaders—especially southern Democrats—score conspicuously low on the party loyalty scale.

One is tempted to assume that the leadership role (or roles) embraces some commitment to party loyalty, a plausible assumption since leaders do not appear to differ in other significant respects from their high-seniority, nonleader colleagues. It is possible, too, that the influence of party leaders over committee assignments may operate to place slightly more loyal members in line for advancement—even given the inexorable workings of seniority. Unfortunately, a definitive explanation must await further investigation.

Still another factor related to party role is the electoral character of the member's constituency. In discussing the effects of seniority on party role, we have already suggested that electoral vulnerability produces dependence upon party, while electoral safety yields independence from party. The extent to which this hypothesis is borne out can be seen in the figures in Table 5-8. As the figures demonstrate, legislators from marginal districts are more apt to be Superloyalists, and those from safe districts are more inclined to be Mavericks. The two groups' centers of gravity, as indicated by average party index scores, are disparate: Congressmen from electorally competitive districts rank higher on the continuum of party loyalty than do their colleagues whose electoral fortunes are more assured.*

Table 5–8. Marginality of District and Party Role Among 86 Congressmen

Role	Marginal	Safe
Superloyalist	36%	13%
Loyalist	24	45
Neutral	27	17
Maverick	12	25
Total	99%	100%
(n)	(33)	(53)
Party Index	2.82	2.46

*Ripley found no persistent relationship between 1962 margin of victory and party loyalty voting. However, when he compared party voting with electoral margin in the next election (1964) he discovered that Democrats who won by the narrowest and widest margins were less loyal than those in the middle. Among Republicans, those who won by very narrow or very large margins in the conservative areas of the South and Midwest tended to be most loyal.[18] As for level of voting in support of the President, district competitiveness does not seem to bear a strong relationship.[19]

The effect of electoral vulnerability is somewhat different in the two political parties. These relationships are set forth in Table 5–9. Democrats and Republicans alike are more apt to assume party-oriented roles if they come from competitive districts. However, the magnitude of the variation is different in the two parties. While marginal Democrats are considerably more oriented to party-centered roles than their colleagues from safe districts, within the Republican party this variation is relatively small. This permits us to assess more completely our earlier finding that Republicans express Superloyalist-Loyalist roles more frequently than Democrats. (See Table 5–3.) A plausible explanation for this phenomenon is found in the impact of electoral marginality and the differing character of Republican and Democratic Congressional districts. For while fully half the Republicans in our sample represented marginal districts, only one third of the Democrats came from such districts.* A substantial part of Democratic "disloyalty" (if the phenomenon can be called that) may be attributed to the fact that so many Democrats face only minimal threat of electoral defeat. Democrats from competitive areas, on the other hand, are among the most loyal Congressmen. On the Republican side of the aisle, the disparity between marginal and safe members (represented in equal numbers in our sample) is relatively narrow.

Table 5–9. Marginality of District, Party Affiliation, and Party Role Among 86 Congressmen

Role	Democrats		Republicans	
	Marginal	Safe	Marginal	Safe
Superloyalist	44%	6%	29%	29%
Loyalist	19	53	29	29
Neutral	25	17	29	18
Maverick	13	25	12	24
Total	101%	101%	99%	100%
(n)	(16)	(36)	(17)	(17)
Party Index	2.96	2.42	2.73	2.63

Armed with these findings on the impact of electoral vulnerability, perhaps we can cast further light on the phenomenon we identified earlier: the inverse relationship of seniority and the

*It has already been observed that these figures closely parallel those for the House as a whole.

level of party loyalty, as revealed by the party role dimension. Could this phenomenon stem from the fact that high-seniority Congressmen come disproportionately from safe constituencies? Of our respondents who had six or more terms of service in the House, all but 18 per cent represented districts classed as safe. By contrast, all but 18 per cent of the first-termers represented marginal districts. Among members with moderate seniority (two to five terms), 61 per cent came from safe districts and 39 per cent from marginal districts. Perhaps it is not the accumulation of seniority itself, but the electoral independence that underlies it, which exerts the crucial impact upon party roles.

Unfortunately, this problem cannot be resolved satisfactorily. The very paucity of low-seniority safe members and high-seniority marginal members virtually precludes statistical generalizations. Even the available data, moreover, yield a somewhat mixed answer to our question. Average party index scores decline steadily with seniority, regardless of the electoral character of the member's district. Among low-seniority (freshmen) and high-seniority (six terms or more) respondents, the degree of electoral risk has a negligible impact upon party role—but the numbers in some of the categories are quite small. And among middle-seniority respondents (two to five terms), those from marginal districts were somewhat more party-oriented than those from safer areas.

Thus, rising seniority by itself probably encourages independence from the claims of party organization and party loyalty. While the impact of electoral risk is less clear, there are not adequate grounds for dismissing this factor entirely. First of all, the experienced Representative undoubtedly views his marginal constituency quite differently than he did when he was an inexperienced first-termer. Having survived several successful re-election campaigns, he is likely to see himself as a relatively independent agent even though his margins of victory remain relatively narrow. As we have already noted, our definition of a safe district may be somewhat rigid at this point; in reality some of the marginal districts represented by high-seniority members should be considered safe—either because one party enjoys a stable but not overwhelming majority, or because the incumbent through hard work or effective campaigning has made the district safe for himself.*

---

*These problems have already been discussed in Chap. 4, p. 136.

For members with six or more terms of service, formal roles as party or committee leaders may further complicate the picture. It has already been ascertained that leadership status is associated with slightly higher party loyalty—a fact which suggests that leadership responsibilities tend to pull the member in the direction of his political party. Thus, the average party index score for leaders (all of whom had at least six terms of service) was noticeably higher than for nonleaders of similar seniority. It seems plausible to speculate, then, that were it not for the intervention of leadership roles within this group, party loyalty scores of high-seniority respondents would be even lower than they are.

Two other factors—region and degree of urbanness—help portray the demography of party loyalty in the House. Southerners of both parties are relatively "disloyal," in terms of the partisan roles they select.* For example, our respondents include no southern Superloyalists of either party. Among southern Democrats, 35 per cent (and 47 per cent of the nonleaders) are classed as Mavericks. The most party-oriented groups are western Democrats (index: 3.24) and midwestern Republicans (index: 3.20); fully half of the latter are Superloyalists. There seems to be no tendency for eastern Republicans to be less loyal than their colleagues from other regions (as Ripley found), although Easterners of both parties range widely over the party loyalty spectrum.

As for district type, in the Democratic party urban Representatives seem the most loyal (index: 2.97), followed by rural and suburban members in that order.[20] Among Republicans, suburban members are the most loyal (index: 3.00), followed by rural and urban members. In no case are the patterns very strong, but it is noteworthy that they follow the conventional centers of gravity for the two parties, urban for the Democratic party and suburban for the Republican.[21] These figures must remain tentative, however, for mixed districts (that is, combinations of urban, suburban, or rural) were eliminated from the analysis.

We can now proceed to draw together the strands of the foregoing analysis. First, a Congressman's party affiliation seems to have

*For the definition of regions used here, see note, p. 44.

a bearing upon the party role he articulates. In general, Republicans are more likely to express the Superloyalist role and Democrats the Maverick role. Some of this partisan variation, however, is attributable to the degree of electoral risk experienced by the member in his home district. Congressmen from competitive districts, where the risk is greatest, are led to seek identification with their political party, as manifested by the Superloyalist and Loyalist roles. Their colleagues from safe districts, in contrast, apparently can afford to take a more independent attitude toward the party's claims on their loyalty. This factor serves to raise the over-all level of party loyalty among our Republicans, half of whom represented marginal districts. By the same token, party loyalty among Democrats is dampened because two thirds of the Democratic members surveyed came from safe districts.

Party role is also related to seniority. Generally speaking, members rank lower on the party loyalty continuum as their seniority increases. First-term Congressmen tend to select Superloyalist and Loyalist roles; none in the present sample are Mavericks. Neutral and Maverick roles are more prevalent among members who have accumulated some seniority in the House. Part of this phenomenon, we have noted, can be explained by the fact that high-seniority Congressmen tend to come from safer districts than do their low-seniority colleagues. However, average party index scores are low even among high-seniority members representing electorally marginal districts—a fact which suggests that repeated electoral success, even in competitive two-party districts, encourages members to take a more independent stance toward the claims of their party. Additionally, we have cautioned that our simple classification of safe and marginal districts may yield an imperfect picture of the high-seniority legislator's perception of his vulnerability at the polls: Although high-seniority Congressmen sometimes encounter electoral defeat after long years of service, they may in fact represent safe districts if they win reelection repeatedly, even though by relatively slender majorities.

Party roles of high-seniority members of Congress are affected by yet another factor, formal leadership status. Generally speaking House leaders—in the committee system as well as in the party hierarchies—are more likely to assume Superloyalist or

Loyalist roles than are Congressmen who lack formal leadership responsibilities. This finding is particularly noteworthy because all the House leaders in our sample had at least six terms of service, and most of them represented safe constituencies. Thus, it is reasonable to speculate that leadership roles (not examined in the present research) embrace a measure of loyalty to the party organization that is absent in the role prescriptions of nonleaders.[22] Very possibly the level of party loyalty would be even lower among high-seniority Congressmen were it not for the intervention of formal leadership roles and their consequent pull in the direction of party loyalty. If leadership were not conferred primarily on the basis of seniority, for example, the "generation gap" between younger party-oriented members and senior Mavericks might be more severe than it now appears.

Finally, we can venture some observations about the relationship of party role to the purposive and representational roles described in the preceding chapters. Given the fact that party role is related to the same variables that affect other types of legislative roles—for example, party affiliation, seniority, leadership status, and electoral vulnerability—the patterns of relationship should be fairly predictable. In almost every instance, this turns out to be the case. The average party index scores (our simple measure of the party role dimension) for each of the role groups described in Chapters 3 and 4 are set forth in Table 5–10.

Among primary purposive role orientations, Tribunes and Ritualists are the only ones appearing in sufficient numbers to permit confident generalizations. Tribunes are a highly diverse group of Congressmen, and their average party index score is close to the average for the entire sample. At the same time, however, their party loyalty is considerably higher than that of Ritualists— a fact that underscores the operation of common political variables upon the two role dimensions. Tribunes tend to be Republican and low in seniority—variables associated also with party orientation. Ritualists, by contrast, tend to be Democrats and higher in seniority. The presence of many leaders among the Ritualists probably serves to minimize the variation—that is, to prevent the Ritualists' average party score from dipping even lower. The remaining purposive roles are too sparsely represented in our sample to permit useful analysis; but in no case do the findings do violence to the general lines of our analysis. And it is at least of passing interest that our lone Opportunist—a first-

Table 5-10. Purposive Roles, Representational Roles, and the Party Role Dimension

Role Type	Average Party Index	Number
Purposive Role		
Opportunist	4.00	(1)
Broker	3.34	(3)
Tribune	2.66	(41)
Inventor	2.36	(6)
Ritualist	2.15	(35)
Representational Style		
Delegate	2.90	(20)
Politico	2.77	(40)
Trustee	2.17	(23)
Representational Focus		
District-oriented	2.70	(37)
District-nation equal	2.92	(24)
Nation-oriented	2.27	(23)
Total Sample of Members	2.61	(86)

term Republican from a marginal district—continued to run true to form by expressing a Superloyalist orientation.

The relation of representational style to party role also reflects the operation of common independent variables. Delegates, who refer to constituency needs or demands in making decisions, score highest on the party index—a fact that underscores the prevalence of this role among low-seniority Congressmen from competitive areas. The Trustees—independent souls who look to their own judgment, conscience, or expertise in making legislative choices—display a weaker commitment to the norm of party loyalty. It will be recalled that Trustees are prevalent among high-seniority, safe-district members. Predictably, Politicos fall in the middle level of party loyalty.

The linkage of representational focus to party role is not so clear. True, district-oriented members are more party-oriented than those members with a nationwide focus. This is to be expected, if one applies a line of reasoning parallel to that used in explaining the relationship of representational style. But respondents expressing a dual nation-district focus actually score highest in party loyalty, when it could be predicted that they would fall somewhere in the middle. This phenomenon eludes satisfactory explanation. It is interesting to note, however, that Democrats in this group are somewhat more party-oriented than Republicans—a fact that runs counter to the usual relationship.* A possible explanation, suggested by closer inspection of the interviews, is that the nation-district focus is held by a large number of low- to middle-seniority Democrats from competitive districts, who espouse party responsibility as a means of furthering liberal policies in their party. A scattering of Democratic leaders also appears in this category. These facts may help account for the fact that the nation-district focus is associated with relatively strong party commitment.

GROUP ROLES: FACILITATORS, RESISTORS, NEUTRALS

Political interest groups—private associations that make claims upon the public through political action—have long held a fascination for observers of legislatures. Journalists and reformers originally viewed pressure groups as sinister manipulators who held in thrall scores of Senators and Congressmen. Somewhat later, interest groups were discovered by scholars who saw in the clash of group interests a representative process of decision-making appropriate for complex, industrialized nations. In this view, legislators were not controlled by powerful organized interests; rather, they were scorekeepers in a "great game of democracy," where interest groups were the major contestants. Legislative decisions, like other public policy decisions, served to record the victories and losses of these competing groups.[24] This notion has often been criticized, and present observers would probably assign interest groups a more modest role.[25] While the activities of interest groups certainly offer a partial explanation of public policy decisions, in relatively few instances can they offer anything approaching a total explanation.

There are several reasons for stressing the limitations upon the legislative influence of interest groups.[26] First, not all sectors of American life are equally organized. Thus, in some important policy areas legislators must act in the absence of evidence that

---

*The fact that district-oriented Republicans express somewhat higher party loyalty than district-oriented Democrats runs counter to another assumption—namely, that the Democratic party is somewhat more flexible in responding to the constituency demands made upon legislators. Here as elsewhere, however, Republicans are more party-oriented than their Democratic colleagues.[23]

citizens are (or might become) organized to express themselves. Second, interest groups do not usually reach most legislators; rather, they have the habit of talking to members who are already committed to their side, or to those who possess expertise in the problems that interest them. Finally, Congressmen are not always receptive to influence, for they have commitments of their own—from their backgrounds or group memberships or constituency interests. They tend to exchange their views with fellow legislators, trading information and opinions without explicitly mentioning interest groups. In this fashion, even issues on which interest groups are active may be discussed and debated on Capitol Hill with little hint of group pressure so far as most members are concerned.

Altogether too much of our knowledge about organized groups in politics rests upon inference. A well-known organization takes a stand on an issue and sets its machinery in motion to lobby on Capitol Hill. Against this backdrop of seemingly furious activity, Congress decides in accord with the group's position. Hence, it is concluded, the group was influential. We infer the fact of influence by noting that the group's lobbying accorded with the Congressional action. But was the group's activity really influential? Would we be forced to conclude otherwise if Congress had acted differently? To reach valid conclusions about the group's influence, we would have to know how the group's message was communicated, what the response was, and whether the response stimulated or reinforced actions consistent with those advocated by the group. Moreover, we would have to account for the numberless times that group-relevant cues were communicated to legislators without the slightest suggestion of pressure—as when the word of a committee specialist is accepted on an issue, or when attitudes are internalized by the members.

Our strategy for studying the place of interest groups in the Congressional process is to try to identify the members' generalized dispositions toward interest groups—their legitimacy, their lobbying activities, and their proper place as carriers of citizens' demands. It is important to caution once again that these attitudes pertain to groups *in general,* and not *specific* groups in *specific* situations. The attitudes of our respondents in the 88th Congress were tapped by three closed-ended statements.[27] Responses of members to the three items are presented in Table 5–11. These questions

Table 5-11. Attitudes of 87 Congressmen
Toward Interest Groups[a]

Item	Agree	Tend to Agree	Undecided	Tend to Disagree	Disagree	No Answer
On the whole, Congress would work better if there were no interest groups and lobbies trying to influence legislation.	6%	9%	2%	41%	39%	2%
Lobbyists and special interests have entirely too much influence in the House.	14%	15%	1%	32%	36%	2%
Under our system of government, every individual should seek to influence his Congressman directly, rather than through interest groups and organizations.	25%	35%	3%	16%	18%	2%

a These items are adapted from John C. Wahlke et al., The Legislative System (New York: John Wiley, 1962), pp. 502–503.

also constituted a scale of attitudes toward interest groups. Our assumption is that Congressmen's general perceptions of interest groups affect the way they approach specific group requests. Therefore, such attitudes constitute an important link in the chain of influence exerted by interest groups in the legislative arena.

Few Congressmen deny the legitimacy of organized interest groups. Only fifteen per cent of our respondents agree with the proposition that Congress would work better without the activities of such groups. And while opinions are divided, a majority of the respondents deny that lobbyists exert undue influence on deliberations of the House of Representatives.* On the efficacy of citizens' participation through organized groups, however, the legislators in our survey expressed considerable reservation. Sixty per cent, in fact, indicated that individuals would do better to express

---

*However, a midwestern Republican, a key leader from a rural district, observed: "Maybe Congress responds too well to pressure groups. People say Congress is not responsive enough, but it's not true."

themselves directly to Congressmen, rather than through organized groups.

While interest groups enjoy general acceptance by members of Congress, their activities run counter to another powerful norm of democratic politics: that citizens should express themselves directly to their elected officials. Perhaps Congressmen simply prefer to do business with individual constituents; perhaps they are more receptive to individually motivated attempts at influence, as opposed to efforts obviously triggered by a directive from some Washington lobbyist. A number of our respondents expressed such sentiments. Whatever the reasons, legislators clearly place high value on the individual citizen's efforts to express himself on public issues. It is significant that this attitude militates more severely against interest-group activity than against participation through political parties. (See Table 5-1.)

To describe the factors associated with these attitudes, we have ranked respondents according to the degree to which their answers were favorable to interest groups. We have then classified the respondents into three groups: "Facilitators," "Neutrals," and "Resistors."* As with our earlier discussion of partisan attitudes, we view these as role perceptions indicating the member's over-all attitude toward interest groups. The distribution of these roles among the eighty-five members whose responses were classifiable is shown in Table 5-12. If an index is constructed from the continuum of group attitudes represented by the three role types, the group index score for the entire sample is 2.06 (on a scale of 3.0).† Thus, the center of gravity in our total sample is the Neutralist role.

Wahlke and his colleagues hypothesized that group roles are in large part a function of the salience of interest groups to the legislative process. Thus they found that Facilitator roles were more

---

*The procedure was identical to that used earlier to determine partisan roles. Each proposition had five gradations of response: agree (with progroup position), tend to agree, undecided, tend to disagree and disagree. (In all instances, the wording of the statements meant that progroup response was actually negative.) Responses to each statement were weighted from 1 (antigroup) to 5 (progroup), then cumulated and averaged for each respondent. Thus a perfect progroup score would be 5.0; a perfect antigroup score 1.0. From the respondents' scores, three groups were drawn: Facilitators (scoring between 4.0 to 5.0); Neutrals (3.0 through 3.7); and Resistors (1.0 through 2.7).

†A simple index score was assigned each respondent on the following basis: Facilitator, 3; Neutral, 2; Resistor, 1. Index scores were then averaged for the population in question—in this case, the total sample of 85.

Table 5-12. Interest-Group Roles Among 85 Congressmen

Facilitator	29%
Neutral	49
Resistor	21
Total	99%
(n)	(85)
Group Index	2.06

prevalent in state legislatures subject to intensive group activity and lobbying; conversely, Resistor roles were more common in states where groups were less active.[28] From the large plurality of Neutralist roles among our Congressional respondents, we would conclude that organized interest groups are only moderately salient in the minds of individual legislators. However, any further inferences—about, for example, the salience of groups in the Congressional process generally—would stretch this datum beyond reasonable limits.

What types of members tend to be most receptive to the claims of organized groups? Which members are most resistant to such claims? If our data are accurate, they should permit a relatively clear statement of some of the over-all conditions for interest-group access to legislators and the legislative arena. While not conclusive, the data provide some tentative answers to these questions—answers which on the whole are consistent with our understanding of legislative role-taking.

The legislator's party affiliation appears to be related to the role he assumes toward interest groups. The initial basis for this conclusion appears in Table 5-13, which indicates that Republicans are more favorably disposed toward interest groups than

Table 5-13. Party Affiliation and Interest-Group Roles Among 85 Congressmen

Role	Democrats	Republicans
Facilitator	24%	38%
Neutral	45	56
Resistor	31	6
Total	100%	100%
(n)	(51)	(34)
Group Index	1.93	2.32

Democrats. Republicans are more apt to appear as Facilitators, and only two could be classed as Resistors. In contrast, almost one third of the Democrats in our general sample are Resistors. The partisan difference is illustrated dramatically in the group index scores, with Republicans scoring considerably above the House average and Democrats slightly below it. This finding, it might be noted, is somewhat inconsistent with that of an earlier study of thirty-four members of the 86th Congress. On the basis of responses to that survey, the researchers concluded that Democrats were more likely to "estimate that organized groups are very important in getting favorable Congressional action. . . ."[29] While it is true that the present survey attempted to measure a somewhat different attitude dimension, it is still not clear (assuming both sets of findings to be valid) why Democrats should assign greater importance to interest groups, at the same time appear more resistant to them.

One explanation for the difference could lie in variations in candidate recruitment. As we discovered in Chapter 2, Republican Congressmen are more frequently drawn from business backgrounds; legal careers, while dominant in both parties, are more so within the Democratic party. Moreover, regardless of previous career, Republican legislators were found to be more geographically mobile than their Democratic colleagues. These earlier findings suggest a possible explanation for the Republicans' relatively favorable attitudes toward interest groups. Conceivably, Republican orientations are an outgrowth of membership in many private associations during the pre-Congressional career.

The data offer little support to this line of reasoning. A Congressman's occupational background makes little difference in the interest-group role he assumes. Although lawyers in both parties are slightly more group-oriented than businessmen, this difference is insignificant compared to the difference *between* the two parties.* Republicans are more prone to see interest groups in a favorable light, regardless of whether they come from business or legal careers. By the same token, Democrats of both occupational groupings are less favorable toward groups. Among members drawn

---

*Lawyers, it has been suggested, should find the Facilitator role particularly congenial because of their training in the brokerage function.[30] Studies of role-taking among state legislators have not borne out the hypothesis, and the present study offers no strong evidence in that direction.[31]

from other occupations, there is no variation between the parties. Differences in occupational background, then, offer no promising explanation of interest-group roles. The impression remains that some critical differences in the parties' recruitment patterns may be operative, even if they do not show up in broad demographic differences between Democratic and Republican legislators.

Other variables must underlie the partisan variance in interest-group roles. For example, formal leadership status in the House—a factor of some usefulness in explaining other legislative roles—might well be operative here. Table 5-14 presents the relationship of party, leadership status, and group role. Quite a different pattern emerges from these figures. Among leaders, there is little difference in the group roles of Republicans and Democrats. Nonleader Democrats, moreover, resemble the two leadership groups. The three groups are broadly similar, on the average only slightly more resistant to interest groups than the entire sample. The fourth group, however, is quite distinct. Republican nonleaders are significantly more group-oriented than their colleagues, with 41 per cent classed as Facilitators and only 3 per cent (one respondent) classed as a Resistor. Though other factors may be associated with interest-group role, clearly we must remain alert to further clues about the characteristics of these Republican nonleaders.

Experience in the legislature would, one would assume, be related to interest-group role. One of the major contributions of groups to the legislative process is information and voting cues on pending issues—commodities sorely needed by the young and inexperienced Congressman. We have already seen that such a member is apt to turn to his party organization for this information. Lacking the expertise, confidence, and contacts to help him obtain such information, he must turn to outside sources. Similarly, we would expect the member's assessment of groups to be related inversely to his length of service.[32] But Wahlke and his colleagues were led to an opposite conclusion from their examination of four state legislatures. In three of the four states, Facilitators were found to have longer average service than Neutrals or Resistors. The investigators thus reasoned that "adjustment of group conflicts" was a norm of institutional purpose to which legislators became socialized with increasing service.[33]

Table 5–14. Leadership, Status, Party Affiliation, and Interest-Group Roles of 113 Congressmen[a]

Role	Leaders			Nonleaders		
	Democrats	Republicans	Total	Democrats	Republicans	Total
Facilitator	26%	24%	25%	27%	41%	33%
Neutral	42	48	45	45	55	49
Resistor	32	29	30	27	3	18
Total	100%	101%	100%	99%	99%	100%
(n)	(19)	(21)	(40)	(44)	(29)	(73)
Group Index	1.94	1.97	1.95	1.98	2.36	2.15

a Leader over-sample groups included.

Our findings, presented in Table 5-15, serve to confirm the former view. In general, rising seniority is accompanied by decreasing receptivity to group claims. And though partisan breakdowns are hazardous because of the small numbers, this phenomenon seems attributable largely to the striking decline among Democrats. The most resistance to interest groups appears among high-seniority Democrats, 50 per cent of whom are Resistors. In the Republican party, however, there is no such shift in interest-group roles; and in fact, experienced Republicans have a slightly more favorable view of groups than do Republican freshmen. These figures again suggest that as a group, Republican members are likely to be receptive to the activities and demands of organized interests.

Table 5–15. Seniority, Party Affiliation, and Interest-Group Roles Among 85 Congressmen

Role	One Term			Members, By Seniority 2–5 Terms			6–Plus Terms		
	Dem.	GOP	Total	Dem.	GOP	Total	Dem.	GOP	Total
Facilitator	57%	30%	41%	25%	40%	31%	13%	44%	21%
Neutral	29	60	47	60	60	60	38	44	39
Resistor	14	10	12	15		9	50	11	39
Total	100%	100%	100%	100%	100%	100%	101%	99%	99%
(n)	(7)	(10)	(17)	(20)	(15)	(35)	(24)	(9)	(33)
Group Index	2.43	2.20	2.29	2.10	2.40	2.22	1.65	2.31	1.80

The member's electoral prospect—whether his district is safe or marginal—is a powerful factor in conditioning representational and party roles. It is one of the most important facts in the Congressman's public life, influencing as it does his responses to many aspects of his environment. If we analyze district character and group role, as in Table 5–16, several interesting patterns emerge. First, as a group, Congressmen from marginal districts are slightly more favorable to interest groups than are members from safe districts. Among the latter, however, Democrats and Republicans show a striking difference. Safe Republicans, it would seem, are extremely receptive to interest group activities—in fact, slightly more so than Republicans from competitive areas. On the other hand, safe Democrats are more resistant to groups, and 40 per cent can be classed as Resistors. And though Republicans in general are more group-oriented than Democrats, it seems clear that this fact again flows largely from the unequal distribution of electoral risk in the two parties—Republicans as a group being more vulnerable electorally than Democrats.

Table 5–16. Marginality of District, Partisan Affiliation, and Interest-Group Role Among 85 Congressmen

Role	Marginal Members			Safe Members		
	Dem.	GOP	Total	Dem.	GOP	Total
Facilitator	25%	24%	24%	23%	53%	33%
Neutral	63	71	67	37	41	38
Resistor	13	6	9	40	6	29
Total	101%	101%	100%	100%	100%	100%
(n)	(16)	(17)	(33)	(35)	(17)	(52)
Group Index	2.14	2.20	2.15	1.73	2.47	2.04

Once again we find that the Congressman's likely fortunes at the polls loom large in determining his role perceptions. Winning by large margins does not, of course, confer immunity to constituency demands, or even to possible defeat in a primary or general election. Nevertheless, it does appear to produce distinctive role orientations. As far as interest groups are concerned, it appears that relative electoral safety is associated in the two parties with quite different responses. For Republicans the norm apparently dictates friendliness to groups and their contribution to the legislative process. For Democrats the norm is one of relative resistance to group influence. These differing norms must surely arise from demographic variations between Republican and Democratic districts. For example, typically Republican districts tend to represent higher levels of socioeconomic status, electoral turnout, home ownership, and white-collar employment. Such districts are presumably more receptive to the norm of interest-group activity than are districts with the opposite characteristics.[34]

The relationships among the various factors we have discussed are difficult to identify, because as more variables are controlled in the analysis, the number of cases in each cell becomes inordinately small. However, some hint of the relationships can be gained by comparing the average group index scores for several groups of respondents. By restricting our attention to high-seniority Congressmen, as in Table 5-17, we may be able to see more clearly the operation of the variables (remembering that as a group these members are somewhat less favorable to interest groups than the House as a whole). Again, we see that Republicans are typically more favorable to interest groups than are Democrats. Republican

Table 5–17. Average Group Index Scores of High-Seniority Congressmen, by Leadership Status, Party Affiliation, and Electoral Risk [a]

Grouping Leaders	Average Index Score	Number
GOP, Marginal	2.00	(9)
GOP, Safe	1.92	(12)
GOP Total	1.97	(21)
Dem., Marginal	3.00	(2)
Dem., Safe	1.83	(17)
Dem. Total	1.94	(19)
Nonleaders		
GOP, Marginal		(0)
GOP, Safe	2.75	(4)
GOP Total	2.75	(4)
Dem., Marginal	1.75	(4)
Dem., Safe	2.14	(14)
Dem Total	1.78	(18)

a Includes leader over-samples.

nonleaders, along with Democratic leaders from marginal districts, seem to be the most progroup in their responses—though the number of respondents in each grouping was quite small. Among the two leadership groups, again, marginal Congressmen are somewhat more favorable to interest groups than are safe Congressmen. This finding does not extend to Democratic nonleaders, but again the numbers of cases in some of the cells are uncomfortably small.

Finally, we shall want to examine the relationship of interest-group roles to the role dimensions described previously. In virtually every respect these patterns—represented in Table 5-18 by average group index scores for each role category—bear a remarkable resemblance to the pattern followed by partisan role perceptions. (See Table 5-10 above.) Indeed, aside from the fact that a four-point scale was used for the party role dimension and a three-point scale for the interest-group dimension, the two tables are virtually the same—a fact that reinforces our growing impression

Table 5–18. Purposive Roles, Representational Roles, and the Interest-Group Role Dimension

Role Category	Average Group Index	Number
Purposive Role		
Opportunist	3.00	(1)
Broker	2.69	(3)
Tribune	2.22	(41)
Ritualist	1.93	(34)
Inventor	1.67	(6)
Representational Style		
Delegate	2.40	(20)
Politico	2.15	(40)
Trustee	1.68	(22)
Representational Focus		
District-oriented	2.35	(37)
District-Nation equal	1.96	(23)
Nation-oriented	1.78	(23)
Partisan Role		
Superloyalist	2.35	(17)
Loyalist	2.04	(31)
Neutral	2.27	(18)
Maverick	1.76	(18)

that a fundamental role-set dichotomy underlies several of the role dimensions we have been describing.*

Among the purposive role groups, the Tribunes and Ritualists are the only roles present in sufficient number to permit confident generalizations. While Congressmen expressing these substantive roles do not fall at the extremes of the interest-group continuum, their relative place in the rankings accords with our understanding of the content of the two roles. (See the discussion in Chapter 2.) Tribunes adhere to the norm of voicing the needs or desires of external constituencies, and they rank somewhat above the House average in responsiveness to interest-group claims. Ritualists, who adhere more closely to the intra-House norms of substantive specialization and committee apprenticeship, score somewhat below the House average in their response to organized interests. While the number of cases in each of the remaining purposive role categories is small, they invariably appear on the scale about where our knowledge of these roles suggests they should appear. Brokers, whose substantive interest in the House is the balancing of interests, express highly favorable attitudes toward interest groups; our single Opportunist, again running true to form, compiled a perfect progroup score. At the other end of the spectrum are the Inventors, whose concern for independent policy entrepreneurship is associated with relatively hostile attitudes toward organized interests.

The two representational role dimensions also offer no surprises. In each case, members who tend to exhibit greatest independence from outside pressures (Trustee, National) seem also most resistant to group influence. Delegate or Local Congressmen, in contrast, exhibit considerable friendliness toward interest groups. In both cases the rankings are similar to those presented in Table 5-10. Hence, we can conclude that representational role perceptions bear a similar relationship to interest-group and party roles. As the legislator perceives himself independent of his district or of external instructions, so he tends to see himself emancipated equally from the claims of party and interest groups. Conversely, Congressmen who are Delegates or Locals tend to express a more favorable disposition both toward party and interest groups.

---

*A close inspection of Tables 5-10 and 5-18 will show that there is, in fact, but one difference in the ranking of purposive and representational role groups. This is the reversal of the Ritualists and Inventors in the two rankings.

This conclusion is generally corroborated by the direct relationship between party and group roles shown in Table 5-18. Although the rankings are not precisely as would be predicted, the over-all direction of the figures is consistent with our assumptions. As expected, Superloyalists are the most group-oriented; Mavericks are the least group-oriented. The group orientations of Loyalists and Neutrals are less clear, although they fall somewhere in the middle of the role continuum. No doubt, therefore, any conclusion concerning the direct relationship of partisan and interest-group roles must be carefully drawn. While the two role dimensions are undoubtedly parallel, other variables may intervene to blur the relationship.

CONCLUSIONS

In the foregoing discussion we have examined the attitudes of Congressmen toward two important features of their legislative environment. Political parties make claims upon the loyalty of every legislator. Interest groups articulate the demands of organized segments of the society. Our sample of Representatives revealed varying responses to these claims upon their loyalty and commitment. We have also examined the factors affecting these responses, in an attempt to describe the conditions surrounding role-taking by members of the House.

If we may generalize from our discussion, it would seem that these two role orientations reflect the legislator's needs for outside assistance—information, voting cues, or other points of reference—in making decisions of often baffling complexity. Those members who are most favorably oriented toward parties and groups—low-seniority and electorally vulnerable members, for example—are apparently more dependent upon these organizations for the cues they need. Members less in need of these commodities are less favorably disposed toward parties and interest groups. This thread runs through the findings we have presented, though there are exceptions to this generalization. First, leaders are more party-oriented than nonleaders, despite the fact that their high seniority and relative electoral safety might otherwise foster independence from partisan claims. Secondly, party affiliation itself seems to exert an independent impact upon party and interest-group roles, Republicans showing themselves slightly more proparty and progroup than Democrats. This variation may be the result of different kinds of constituencies, or of divergent patterns of intra-House socialization.

Finally, party and interest-group roles appear to be part of a larger framework of role conceptions—a framework that embraces both purposive and representational orientations. Consistency and conflict among the various role dimensions will be the subject of the concluding chapter.

CHAPTER 6

THE STRUCTURE OF LEGISLATIVE ROLES

In trying to describe the complexities of a human system like the United States Congress, the social scientist is bound to leave many questions unanswered, many paths of inquiry unexplored. He might choose to treat his subject at a low level of generalization, describing in minute fashion the institution, its Members, its behavior, or its environment. This strategy has the virtues of precision in detail and richness of elaboration; yet too often it lacks adequate strands to weave a whole picture.

In this book we have followed a second strategy. By employing the role concept, we have been able to draw a generalized job description for the U.S. Representative. The result has been a wholistic picture of the interaction of legislators with their environment.

The over-all job description we have drawn for the Representative is, on the whole, a remarkably coherent portrait. Members of Congress, like legislators at other levels of our federal system, express a limited number and range of orientations toward their tasks. Even our incomplete catalog of role dimensions indicates that role analysis offers a fruitful perspective for characterizing the legislator's job. Role cognitions, moreover, are related in relatively systematic fashion to commonly understood political variables—for example, to electoral risk and degree of intra-House socialization. Role cognitions, then, are meaningful, patterned responses to the environment in which legislators must function. In turn, these cognitions are undoubtedly closely linked to the multitude of specific decisions these same legislators must reach from day to day.

Our concluding discussion will summarize some of the more salient characteristics of members' role cognitions, chart the over-all structure of role-taking in the House, and suggest the possible points of conflict between these roles and the expectations of relevant publics.

A ROLE TAXONOMY

Members of the contemporary House of Representatives are a distinctive and relatively homogeneous group of men and women. They are recruited from the same small number of relatively privileged occupations. Invariably they have served a prolonged apprenticeship in local politics. And if they possess common or similar pre-Congressional careers, they share even more the Washington experience. They are faced with a demanding work schedule; they work in an uncertain environment and must cope with problems that are understood, if not shared, by all members. Yet the rewards of office are considerable, in psychological if not monetary terms; and today's Congressman is apt to consider his office not only a full-time responsibility, but a unique and prestigious career. In other words, the House comprises a true group—perhaps more so than at any time in its history.

At the same time, Congressmen are transplanted citizens. Prior to their election, they are almost certain to have enjoyed long association with their state or district. Most are prominent citizens in their communities long before they aspire to Congress. Democratic theory reinforces this element of localism, for the Representative is the electorate's fiduciary agent in the nation's capital. If he need not reflect the constituency's wishes on each and every issue, nonetheless he cannot ignore its will (when it is expressed) with impunity. The electorate wields the ultimate sanction—a blunt instrument perhaps, and less frequently used now than in earlier times—of retiring a member who conspicuously or repeatedly neglects his obligations to the people back home.

In terms of the role performance expected of him, the legislator is a divided soul. Some forces draw him into the legislature, others pull him away. He is a local at heart, but institutional work patterns draw him into the Capitol Hill milieu. He is constituency-oriented, but he is also task- and work-group-oriented. The roles that the Capitol Hill system requires of him may conflict with the roles constituents expect of him. Thus, the legislator—and the fiduciary function generally—is at the core a set of conflicting role-demands. Speaking institutionally, Congress as a system of roles is a "mediate" structure. David B. Truman's characterization of the Congressional party is equally applicable to Congress itself: The role-demands of the institution upon its members are "mediate and supplementary rather than immediate and inclusive."[1] Some expectations, then, originate within the institution as a grouping of interacting men and women; other expectations emanate from systems outside Congress—from constituencies in particular, but from many other sources as well.

The dual character of the legislator's status—as member of a viable and prestigious group, and as spokesman for external interests—creates an essentially dual structure of roles. Effective performance of group-centered roles does not, for example, insure success at the polls. Conversely, successful cultivation of a constituency does not insure skillful or influential performance in the committee rooms or on the floor. Like their colleagues in the Senate, members of the House may be Insiders or Outsiders.[2] Some members fuse both roles; others stress one or the other.

Several factors work to keep this role conflict in bounds. First, neither the norms of the institution nor the expectations of external publics are so inflexible as to preclude a large range of individualized performance. The folkways of legislatures are invariably tolerant; they implicitly acknowledge that fiduciaries must strike hard bargains, and they are designed to minimize the divisiveness that can flow from this fact. Nor are constituencies as insistent as they may appear at first glance. Politicians claim to believe that voters are always asking, "What have you done for us lately?" But the fact that voters have to ask the question suggests they are not always paying attention. Their memory, needless to add, may be as short as their attention span.

Moreover, at any given point in time, members of the House face widely varying levels of role expectations. Perhaps the most conspicuous example is the differing levels of demands that constituencies make upon Representatives. To paraphrase Franklin D. Roosevelt: To some members much is given, from others much is expected. Some legislators are fortunate enough to represent relatively undemanding electorates—one-party or demographically homogeneous areas with a narrow core of policy interests. These legislators do not necessarily have a blank check to do with what they wish; but their range of permissible behavior is very broad, providing they do not forget the core of orthodoxy that the constituency demands. The relatively low level of demands thus confers a large amount of objective freedom so that the member can concentrate upon, and perhaps master, the internal roles of the House.

Other members have less freedom to pursue institution-based roles. Their districts are competitive and two-party, or embrace a heterogeneous mixture of interests, or contain local political organizations that must be nurtured constantly. The "cracker-ass Congressman," whose competitive district offers him little respite, is one kind of House Outsider; the "Tuesday-to-Thursday Club" member, who returns to his district every weekend, is another.

Finally, the relative salience of internal and external role expectations undoubtedly varies with time. Contemporary Congressmen, for example, are more firmly "House men" than their nineteenth-century predecessors. In virtually every respect, today the institution itself makes heavier demands and offers greater rewards. By comparison, a secular decline in the competitiveness of districts has probably served to moderate external role-expectations, while developments in transportation, communication, and staff assistance may have rendered these demands less burdensome to perform. This is not to say that contemporary Representatives are Insiders or Nationals, and not Outsiders or Locals. But internal and external roles are probably in greater equilibrium today than in the past.

Those who criticize Congressmen as anomalous provincials may be comparing them with other, more cosmopolitan elite groups, or with some a priori standard of what it means to be "broad gauged" (to use the businessman's term) in responding to contemporary problems. But such arguments may be historically misleading. Needless to say, historical data on role-taking are lacking; but changing career patterns as well as qualitative evidence give substance to the conclusion that task- and group-centered roles are more prevalent today than ever before.

The Congressmen we interviewed exhibited relatively limited and coherent sets of role prescriptions. Yet there is sufficient conflict among roles to suggest something of the mediate and contingent character of the legislative system. In terms of the model of legislative behavior introduced in Chapter 1, the Insider-Outsider conflict is a reflection of the somewhat precarious bonds of a group in which a number of crucial goals and resources are unshared and shaped by external forces.

The dualism of forces is illustrated by purposive role orientations. The two dominant roles, Tribune and Ritualist, are reasonably comprehensive descriptions of the *substantive* content of the Outsider and Insider functions. The Tribune approaches the classic understanding of the legislator-as-representative: the reflector, articulator, champion of the needs or wishes of external publics. Regardless of his style of representation, regardless of the particular constituency to which he is attuned, the Tribune sees himself as the carrier of external demands. The Tribune orientation is so widespread among our respondents that it must be considered virtually a consensual view of the minimum requirements of the legislator's job. Thus, we have utilized the distinction between primary and secondary roles to distinguish between Tribunes and holders of other purposive roles.

By contrast, the Ritualist orientation is a cogent characterization of the Insider's concerns—the Congressman as legislative specialist, substantive expert, procedural manipulator, or party chieftain. The Ritualist most nearly approximates the norms of internal House advancement—the "seniority-protégé-apprenticeship system," as Richard F. Fenno has termed it.[3] The late Speaker Sam Rayburn, the patron saint of Congressional Ritualists, articulated many of the facets of this orientation in his advice to Capitol Hill newcomers:

> Those who are members of a committee for a long time learn the problems before the committee and become good leaders.
>
> It takes a while for a man to learn, and get established, and gain his full influence. He doesn't reach his full usefulness in his first term or two. And the worst thing a district can do for itself, if it's got someone here doing the job right, is to keep changing its congressman. A man makes a record in the House the way he does in business or the law or anywhere else. It's hard work that makes the difference.
>
> If you want to *get* along, *go* along.[4]

The Ritualist orientation, and the norms of behavior associated with it, are little different from the Insider's view of accepted Senatorial behavior—Donald R. Matthews' "effective Senator," for example, or William S. White's member of the "Inner Club." [5]

It should not be supposed that the Tribune is unconcerned with the inner workings of the House, nor that the Ritualist is unresponsive to the duties of an elected representative. But the emphases of the two purposive orientations are different. Moreover, different kinds of members tend to assume these two roles as primary purposive orientations. Tribunes are over-represented in the ranks of freshmen, nonleaders, Republicans, legislators with business backgrounds (and, to a lesser extent, combinations of law and other occupations). Ritualists are disproportionately leaders, Democrats, senior members, and lawyers. Selection of this purposive role, as noted in Chapter 3, is primarily a reflection of the member's socialization in the House.

Other purposive roles—Inventor, Broker, Opportunist—appear in fewer numbers among our sample. The natures of these roles, as well as the characteristics of members assuming them, suggest that they too fit into the Insider-Outsider dichotomy. Inventors are essentially Insiders; Opportunists are Outsiders par excellence. Brokers, almost by definition, are middlemen in this play of forces.

The Congressman's *style* and *focus* of representation provide even clearer evidence of the pervasive duality of legislative roles. Though the two dimensions are analytically separate, they are closely related. The stylistic distinction rests on whether the legislator sees himself as acting upon his own knowledge, understanding, or conscience (Burke's Trustee), or whether he sees himself as mirroring the sentiments of external clienteles (the instructed Delegate). Of course, all Congressmen play both roles as the circumstances demand. In this sense, they are all Politicos. The exigencies of the legislator's environment constrain him to play off his own initiatives against the demands others make of him, acting on instructions one moment and on his own the next. But again, most of our respondents were able to verbalize important and persistent variations in emphasis. Moreover, different types of Congressmen are attracted to the diverging styles of representation. A summary of our findings, utilizing the simple three-point Delegate-to-Trustee scale introduced in Chapter 4, is presented in Table 6-1.

The member's focus of representation, too, varies with the level of demands made upon him. One legislator may take essentially a national view of his tasks (again, Burke's National), while another plays the role of the archetypical Local. A few members are atten-

Table 6-1.
Representational Styles
of Congressmen: A Summary

Style	Grouping
TRUSTEE (3.00)	
	Inventors (2.67)
	Party Mavericks (2.46)
	Group Resistors (2.44)
	Ritualists (2.38)
	Leaders (2.31)
	Safe Members (2.24)
	High-Seniority Members (2.20)
	Middle-Seniority Members (2.11)
	Democrats (2.11)
	Party Neutralists (2.07)
	Group Neutralists (2.02)
POLITICO (2.00)	Brokers (2.00)
	HOUSE MEDIAN (1.99)
	Party Loyalists (1.93)
	Republicans (1.92)
	Party Superloyalists (1.86)
	Nonleaders (1.85)
	Marginal Members (1.75)
	Group Facilitators (1.71)
	Tribunes (1.70)
	Freshmen (1.57)
DELEGATE (1.00)	Opportunists (1.00)

tive to nongeographic functional constituencies, either because their districts embrace the interests of similar groupings in other geographic regions, or because their committee responsibilities embrace a definable but geographically scattered constituency. Again, few if any Congressmen play a single role consistently—if only because no partial constituency can ever guide the member's choices on all issues. The ranking of House subgroups on the National-Local continuum is summarized in Table 6-2, which utilizes the three-point area-focus scale introduced in Chapter 4. In most respects the Trustee and National roles are comparable, as are the Delegate and Local roles. In a few cases variables affect the two dimensions differently. (For example, seniority is positively correlated with the Trustee style, but not with National focus; leadership, on the other hand, is related to National focus but not to the Trustee style.) The greatest single determinant of members' representational roles is the level of electoral risk they face in their districts— though other factors exert some influence.

Table 6–2.
Representational Foci
of Congressmen: A Summary

Focus	Grouping
NATIONAL (3.00)	Inventors (2.83)
	Trustees (2.54)
	Ritualists (2.25)
	Group Resistors (2.23)
	Leaders (2.17)
	Politicos (2.03)
NATIONAL-DISTRICT (2.00)[a]	Brokers (2.00)
	Group Neutralists (1.99)
	Safe Members (1.98)
	Democrats (1.97)
	Middle-Seniority Members (1.92)
	Party Mavericks (1.88)
	Party Loyalists (1.87)
	High-Seniority Members (1.86)
	HOUSE MEDIAN (1.84)
	Nonleaders (1.82)
	Party Neutralists (1.79)
	Republicans (1.66)
	Marginal Members (1.66)
	Freshmen (1.62)
	Party Superloyalists (1.60)
	Tribunes (1.47)
	Group Facilitators (1.44)
	Delegates (1.10)
DISTRICT (1.00)	Opportunists (1.00)

a Includes respondents with nongeographic focus.

The Congressman's general orientation toward his political party and toward the claims of organized interests also bears relation to the latitude given him by his electorate. In the main, electoral freedom leads to perceived independence from the claims of parties and interest groups. Freshmen, Delegates, Locals, and those

members from competitive districts all rank above the House
median in party loyalty. Respondents with the opposite characteristics tend to rank below the House median in loyalty. House
leaders are a conspicuous exception to this generalization. Despite
the fact that their attributes—high seniority, for example, and
safe constituencies—would normally pull them away from loyalist
roles, they are relatively loyal to their political parties. In contrast,
high-seniority nonleaders are among the least loyal members in
the House. This striking dichotomy among higher-seniority Congressmen no doubt reflects divergent career patterns within the
House.

Table 6–3.
Partisan Roles of
Congressmen: A Summary

Partisan Role	Grouping
SUPERLOYALIST (4.00)	Opportunists (4.00)
	Brokers (3.34)
LOYALIST (3.00)	Freshmen (2.97)
	District-National Focus (2.92)
	Delegates (2.90)
	Leaders (2.83)
	Marginal Members (2.82)
	Politicos (2.77)
	Middle-Seniority Members (2.72)
	District Focus (2.70)
	Republicans (2.69)
	Tribunes (2.66)
	HOUSE MEDIAN (2.61)
	Nonleaders (2.61)
	Democrats (2.53)
	Safe Members (2.46)
	Inventors (2.36)
	High-Seniority Members (2.28)
	National Focus (2.27)
	Trustees (2.17)
	Ritualists (2.15)
NEUTRAL (2.00)	
MAVERICK (1.00)	

Table 6–4.
Interest-Group Roles
of Congressmen: A Summary

Group Role	Grouping
FACILITATOR (3.00)	Opportunists (3.00)
	Brokers (2.69)
	Delegates (2.40)
	District Focus (2.35)
	Party Superloyalists (2.35)
	Republicans (2.32)
	Freshmen (2.29)
	Party Neutrals (2.27)
	Tribunes (2.22)
	Middle-Seniority Members (2.22)
	Nonleaders (2.15)
	Marginal Members (2.15)
	Politicos (2.15)
	Party Loyalists (2.04)
	HOUSE MEDIAN (2.04)
	Safe Members (2.01)
NEUTRAL (2.00)	
	National-District Focus (1.96)
	Leaders (1.95)
	Democrats (1.93)
	Ritualists (1.93)
	High-Seniority Members (1.80)
	National Focus (1.78)
	Party Mavericks (1.76)
	Trustees (1.68)
	Inventors (1.67)
RESISTOR (1.00)	

As a rule, Congressmen who take party loyalist roles are also favorably disposed toward the activities of interest groups. Party affiliation is fairly strongly associated with interest-group role: Republicans are more apt to assume pro-group roles than are Democrats. Low seniority, lack of formal leadership position, and competitiveness of district are also related to progroup roles. The relationships of variables to interest-group roles are summarized in Table 6–4, which utilizes the simple index developed in Chapter 5. Interest-group role, as defined here, offers only a general indication of the member's disposition toward interest groups, and we have cautioned that the role may not be applicable to specific interest groups. A progroup legislator may be quite opposed to the work of a particular organization; conversely, a Resistor may in actuality be a spokesman for a particular interest.

As this summarization makes clear, the various role dimensions we have uncovered are not discrete or unrelated phenomena. They reflect coherent and consistent patterns of role-taking, and serve once again to indicate the ordered quality of legislators' attitudes. The "typical" role patterns, as we have described them, are represented in Table 6–5. Of course, our previous discussions have indicated that many individual legislators assume combinations of roles different than the "typical" combinations portrayed here. However, the various role cognitions *tend* to appear in predictable patterns; and, what is more, political variables tend to affect the various role components in similar ways.

Table 6–5.
"Typical" Role Patterns
in the House of Representatives
Role Dimension

Representation

		Style	Focus	Partisan	Interest Group
	Purposive				
	Inventor	Delegate	National	Neutral-Plus	Neutral-Resistor
	Ritualist	Trustee	National	Neutral	Neutral-Minus
Role	Broker	Politico	Natl.-Dist.	Loyalist-Plus	Facilitator
	Tribune	Delegate	District	Loyalist	Neutral-Plus
	Opportunist	Delegate	District	Superloyalist	Facilitator

Table 6–5 has been arranged to show graphically the pervasiveness of the Insider-Outsider dichotomy among members of the House. Insider orientations are found at the top of the diagram, and Outsider roles are found toward the bottom. In other words, the role patterns are shown in descending order of the strength of role expectations emanating within the legislature itself, and in ascending order of the salience of expectations by outside publics or clienteles. As can be seen, Congressmen who are found at a given point on one role dimension are likely to take analogous

roles on the remaining dimensions. Each column, of course, represents a distinct role dimension; and some of the roles are derived through different methods. (The first three columns were coded from open-end responses; the last two columns were scaled categories of closed-end responses.)

Ironically enough, the Inventor appears to be the modern Burkean: the legislator who sees himself as the representative of the national constituency. His party loyalty is moderate—somewhere between the Neutral and Loyalist roles—and he is relatively resistant to interest groups and associations. The Ritualist is the classic "House man"; he is the workhorse of the institution, laboring in the shadow of those legislators whom the House glorifies—the Sam Rayburns, the George Mahons, and the Wilbur Millses, who, whether known outside Washington or not, are nonetheless among the most highly respected Insiders in national politics.

In the balance between internal and external role expectations, the Broker is poised at the center. He is both a Burkean Trustee and an instructed Delegate; he is both National and Local in orientation; and he tends to be receptive to the activities of party and of interest associations.

Tribunes and Opportunists reflect the fact that, while the House is more an autonomous system of behaviors than perhaps at any point in previous history, as an institution it is very much exposed to the outside society (or, literally, to other systems of behavior). The Tribune is an instructed Delegate, a Local, and a party Loyalist; he is slightly more receptive to interest groups than the average Congressman. The prevalence of the Tribune role in the House—it was expressed in some form by more than four out of five respondents—reflects the persistence of democratic norms of representation as well as the presence of constituency pressures. Even Speaker Rayburn, the quintessential Ritualist, was moved to remark:

> I am just a little way from Flag Springs [his birthplace]. You know, I just missed being a tenant farmer by a gnat's whisker.[6]

The Opportunist is (from the point of view of the House) the most marginal man of all: He is a Local and an instructed Delegate par excellence, and he is a friend of both the political party and organized interests.

ROLE CONSENSUS AND CONFLICT

In setting forth the various interpretations of the Representatives' tasks, it is perhaps inescapable that we emphasize the variety of role cognitions, and in particular the potential conflict between Insider and Outsider within the institution. Yet equally noteworthy is the wide spectrum of agreement among all incumbents as to what it means (or ought to mean) to hold the position of United States Representative. We have repeatedly noted, therefore, that role cognitions serve as a distinguishing mark of the legislator, setting him off, as it were, from other political actors and from the general body of citizens.

The role cognitions of incumbents thus reveal the group character of Congress. In each of the role dimensions we have described, the orientations of our respondents encompass a limited range of relatively explicit categories. While any composite picture of the legislators' orientations would be an oversimplification, it can certainly be observed that the average Representative recognizes primarily the centrality of representation (Tribune), and secondarily the need for internal legislative work (Ritualist). As a representative, the average member is a Politico and a Local. Needless to add, the House is not a body of revolutionaries: There are no Agitators (and even few Inventors) among our sample.

If role is an aspect of status, then it is inevitable that the Representatives view their jobs similarly, and in a distinctive fashion. In a demographic sense, the members of the House are a unique group of people. To be sure, the door to Congressional office is probably as open today as it has ever been. The growth of regional economic diversity, as well as a decline in what we have called the Founding Fathers syndrome, has contributed to a broadening of the recruitment base. Yet if anything, Congressional life has become more rigid and institutionalized. Today's Representatives (and Senators as well) tend to follow a career that is distinct from other ladders of political advancement; they are apt to make a career out of legislative service; and they are not inclined to move laterally to alternative jobs, political or otherwise. Professionalization has undoubtedly fostered institutional cohesion on Capitol Hill; whether it has also produced institutional rigidity and insularity is an unanswered question.

While any historical projection of legislative role-taking is bound to be hazardous, it is interesting to speculate on probable trends. What we have discovered concerning the professionalization of legislative office, in particular, suggests that long-term development has been in the direction of internally based roles, such as the Ritualist, that revolve about the activities and procedures of the legislative body itself. To be sure, our respondents display an expected consensus on the Tribune component of their jobs. The historical importance of this role suggests that it has always been the central part of legislators' self-descriptions. The Ritualist and perhaps the Inventor roles, in contrast, are in all probability more recent developments—correlates of heightened institutional cohesion and complexity of public issues. Among representational roles, we might speculate that the historical trend has been toward Trustee and National roles.

The rise of Insider roles, if this has occurred, is highly functional for the maintenance of Congress as a system that is internally cohesive. Such roles betoken an institution that commands the loyalty of its members and is resistant to intrusions upon its prerogatives. Such roles also imply a task-oriented body which has prepared itself to process very large amounts of complicated business items. These statements are relatively descriptive of the Congress of the late twentieth century. What is not so clear is whether this institutional cohesion has been purchased at the price of responsiveness to the demands of the democratic electorate. Such would be the case if the Outsider purposive and representational orientations were insufficiently strong to satisfy the expectations of outside publics.

The evidence concerning this potential role-conflict is far from conclusive. For example, virtually nothing is known about public expectations for the performance of legislators. Given the lack of clarity with which the public views Congress, it is unlikely that the average citizen holds elaborate notions of how his elected Representatives should perform.[7] Representatives themselves frequently lament the voters' failures to understand their jobs and their problems—although lack of public concern (here as elsewhere) tends to shield legislators from intense public demands. If all citizens were concerned about all public issues, the Congressman's lot would indeed be an unhappy one. At the same time, however, the absence of clear instructions from the electorate brings its own problems for the legislator, because it heightens uncertainty over probable public repercussions.

Broadly speaking, the public seems to view elected legislators as servants of the people rather than as policy experts.[8] Thus, citizens apparently expect their Representatives to follow instructions rather than exercise independent judgment.[9] In this respect, public expectations may conflict somewhat with the norms of incumbents, who give rather more weight to independent judgment (the Trustee roles). Again, this conflict is not normally serious, as long as the range of issues for which this expectation is operative remains narrow.[10] Attentive publics pose a thornier problem to legislators than do the larger masses of inattentive citizens: Not only are the "attentives" concerned about a broader range of issues, but they seem more likely than others to expect the legislator to be a Delegate. It is doubtful whether relevant publics harbor any explicit conceptions of the legislators' purposive roles; but citizens probably see the elected official as a representative who should (to the extent that issues are salient) follow the district's instructions in making choices.

At the same time, however, rising educational level and media exposure of the electorate may yield more stringent expectations concerning legislative performance. While the Representative is more than ever the prisoner of Capitol Hill life, he is neither electronically nor psychologically far removed from his constituents. Indeed, the linkages may be closer than in an earlier day, when the government in Washington was "at a distance and out of sight."[11] As the developing institution pulls the member inward, so these continuing demands from external publics force him to look outward. A creative tension between these forces would enhance the vitality and viability of Congress. It is unlikely that today's Congress can survive without solving the dual problems of internal cohesion and external responsiveness. For the future health of the national legislature, the overriding question is whether its members will be capable of mediating this role conflict and the tensions it engenders.

Appendix: Methodology of the Sample Survey

The data presented in Chapters 3 through 6 of this book were derived from personal interviews with members of the House of Representatives in the 88th Congress (1963–1964). The research project was sponsored by the Public Affairs Center of Dartmouth College and was under the co-directorship of Professor David M. Kovenock, now of the University of North Carolina; Professor Michael K. O'Leary, now of Syracuse University; and the author. The survey was designed to provide systematic information concerning Congressional views of the normative and enacted roles of Congress and Congressmen, and a systematic analysis of the politics of Congressional reorganization. A complete exposition of the methodology of the study as it related to the problem of Congressional reorganization has appeared in a previous study co-authored by the principal investigators,[1] and the data were subsequently deposited with the Inter-University Consortium for Political Research, where they are now available to interested students.

SAMPLE DESIGN

That an undertaking of this type might be both fruitful and feasible was suggested by the role-oriented research on state legislatures completed by John C. Wahlke and his associates, as well as by the success of James A. Robinson and of Warren E. Miller and Donald E. Stokes in their attempts to interview sizable samples of Congressmen by means of structured survey instruments.[2] Practical and theoretical considerations led us to limit the survey to the House of Representatives. First, previous personal experience and the findings of other investigators suggested that Representatives would be more accessible to scholars than would Senators. Second, the anticipated use of multivariate analytical techniques required that the sample size approach, if not exceed, one hundred cases; and the available financial resources dictated that the sample be limited to approximately that figure. To have included Senate interviews would have precluded analysis of attitudes internal to the House.

Within the House of Representatives, three samples of members were developed. The first of these has been referred to as the "general" sample. It consisted of eighty-seven completed interviews, stratified by party and by leadership position within the party so that (1) the completed sample had the same ratio of Democrats to Republicans as the House as a whole; and (2) the proportion of leaders and nonleaders interviewed (within each party grouping) was the same as that actually existing in the House.* Respondents within each of these four groups (Democratic and Republican leaders and nonleaders) were chosen on a random basis from a list of all members of the House.

Because formal leadership position (and the closely related factor of seniority) was presumed to be critical for an analysis of legislative role-taking, and because the general sample contained an appropriately small number of formal leaders, it was decided to interview two additional groups of House leaders. First, we interviewed a "leadership over-sample" of 23 members holding leadership positions. In addition to the 110 respondents in these two samples, we interviewed the 6 Representatives in the "top leadership" of both parties who had not been selected for interviewing in either of the two random sampling procedures.† These leadership

*Those members classified as leaders were respondents holding one or more of the following positions in the 88th Congress: Legislative or Appropriations Committee chairmen and ranking minority members; chairmen and ranking minority members of the subcommittes of the Appropriations Committee; the Speaker, Majority Leader, and Majority Whip; and the Minority Leader, Minority Whip, and the Chairman of the Republican Conference (Caucus).

† Top formal leaders included the chairmen and ranking minority members of the committees on Appropriations, Ways and Means, and Rules, as well as the Speaker, Majority Leader, and Majority Whip, and the Minority Leader, Minority Whip, and Republican Conference Chairman.

over-samples, when combined with the general-sample respondents holding leadership positions, provided enough cases to permit analysis of differences in role cognitions within the House leadership group.

The composition of the three samples is summarized in Table A-1. To produce these 116 completed interviews, stratified according to the appropriate party and leadership ratios, it was necessary to draw somewhat larger panels of potential respondents. A total of 132 Representatives was selected for interviewing. Of these,

Table A–1. Summary of the Three Completed Samples of House Members, 88th Congress

Sample		Democrats	Republicans	Sample Totals
General	(nonleaders)	45	29	87
	(leaders)	8	5	
Leadership over-sample		10	13	23
Top-leadership over-sample		3	3	6
Party totals		66	50	116

118 (or 89.4 per cent) were actually interviewed.* As one might suspect, completion rates were not uniform for the four groups of respondents. As Table A-2 indicates, Republicans were somewhat more responsive to our requests for interviews than Democrats— though the latter could hardly be deemed uncooperative. Only among Democrats, moreover, did we actually experience difficulty in gaining access to Representatives holding party- and committee-leadership positions. No systematic differences that would affect the analysis can be discerned between the Democratic leaders we were able to interview and those we were not.

Table A–2. Interview-Panel Completion Rates, by Party and Leadership Position

	Democrats	Republicans	Number in Original Panel
Nonleaders	90%	97%	81
Leaders	75%	96%	51
Number in original panel	78	54	132

* Two of the interviews completed for the random sample were excluded from analysis because they would have served to over-represent one of the party and leadership groups in the sample.

Many tactics were employed to obtain the interviews. Initially, a letter of introduction and explanation was sent to each member whose name had been drawn for one of the samples. One of the principal investigators would then make personal contact with the member's chief assistant, in order to arrange an interview with the Representative. In a majority of cases, this procedure sufficed. In a few instances where no definite arrangements could be made—even after several telephone or personal contacts—we lobbied for access by asking a friendly member to intercede for us. But for the most part we relied upon the hospitality and goodwill of the Congressmen—in combination with our own patience and persistence.

Virtually all interviewing was carried out in the privacy of the members' inner offices. Occasionally, interviews were conducted in the Rayburn reception room adjacent to the floor of the House, or over a meal in one of the House restaurants. Interviews varied in length from twenty minutes to more than four hours, with the mean being around fifty-five minutes. It is estimated that more than five hundred man-hours were consumed in the process of arranging and conducting the 118 interviews.

More than two thirds of the interviews were conducted during the summer of 1963; the rest were obtained during brief visits to Washington that fall, and in the winter and spring of 1964. More than half of the interviews were conducted by one or another of the principal investigators; another 10 per cent were conducted by our research assistant, James M. Hollabaugh. The rest of the interviewing was done by Dartmouth students serving as interns in Washington during the summer of 1963.

THE INTERVIEW SCHEDULE

This study bears a heavy intellectual debt to John C. Wahlke, Heinz Eulau, William Buchanan, and LeRoy C. Ferguson. To their pioneering study of four state legislatures is owed our theoretical orientation and, in a number of cases, the specific wording of the questions designed to elicit the role perceptions of Congressmen.[3] Other items in the survey instrument were designed to elicit members' perceptions of the problems Congress faces, as well as their assessments of various proposals for reform. These latter aspects of the survey have been detailed in a previous report of our research.[4]

An early draft of the survey instrument was pretested during one week in April 1963. We discussed the questions in some detail with a number of Congressional aides and with a varied group of Congressmen.

Here reproduced is the main body of the survey instrument—omitting only the items designed to obtain the respondents' opinions concerning specific proposals for Congressional reforms. On the face sheet were recorded the interview number, the interviewer's name, and the date and length of the interview. Also appearing on this sheet was an explanation of the study, which the interviewer was instructed to relate but not read to the respondent. Following this introduction, the interview embraced these items (with interviewer instructions enclosed in brackets):

1. I'd like to start by asking a couple of questions about the job of being a Congressman:
   a. First of all, how would you describe the job of being a Congressman—what are the most important things you should do here? [*Probe as fully as possible. If there is a difference between what he does and what he thinks he should be doing, explore adequately and get both. If no indication of such, probe to see if ideal and actual roles are in harmony.*]
   b. Now, what are the most pressing problems you face in trying to do your job as Congressman—what are the things that hinder you in your tasks? [*Try to get beyond such general statements as "lack of time"; get the specific things which prevent R from doing his job the way he would like to.*]
2. Now let's turn briefly to the role of Congress *as a whole* and its place in our government:
   a. First, what role should Congress play in our governmental system—what should its functions be? [*Probe as fully as possible. We are anxious to get at perceptions of the role of Congress vis-à-vis the President in legislation and administration, and in regard to the representative functions of Congress. Probe also for perceptions of the role of the House as opposed to the Senate.*]
   b. How effective is Congress (and especially the House) in fulfilling the role(s) you feel it should play? [*Probe to get specific failures of Congress, if R has any on his mind.*]
   c. [*If R sees any discrepancy between what Congress ought to do and what it does:*] What are the most pressing problems which prevent Congress from doing what you think it ought to do?
3. To go a little further with this question, we have collected some statements that Congressmen and others have made about the

nature of Congressional life. You may very well find some of these to be quite oversimplified, particularly since they deal with complex subjects. But we would like your general reaction to each one. These are all matters of opinion so there are no correct or incorrect answers. [*Hand R question 3.*] Would you please read each statement and then check the response which best indicates your agreement or disagreement with the statement. (Note: respondents could choose among "agree," "tend to agree," "undecided," "tend to disagree," and "disagree.")

[Note: See below for the twenty-six items included in this question.]

4. Here is a short list of proposals that Congressmen and others have made for possible changes in congressional organization and procedure. Some of these proposals may seem to you to be radical; others may sound helpful; some may seem trivial. We are anxious to get your reactions to all these proposals. [*Hand R booklet containing question 4.*] Please read each of the proposals in the list and circle your impressions on the two scales which accompany each proposal. If you have any further comments on these proposals I'd be glad to hear them as you go along.

[Note: There followed a list of thirty-two reform proposals, for which the respondent was asked to indicate his own attitude and his estimate of likelihood of adoption. See footnote 4.]

5. [*After R has completed question 4:*] Are there any other specific changes *not* on this list which you would like to mention— either changes you favor or those which you have heard about but do not favor? [*If R mentions any other reforms:*] Using the same scales as appear on the list, what position would you probably take on the proposal? How likely is the House to adopt this proposal within the next ten years?

6. Have you personally discussed with any of your colleagues here in the House any of the proposals on the list (or any of those you have added)?
   [*If "yes":*]
   a. Which proposals were involved?
   b. Who was involved in the discussion?
   c. What was said?
   d. What has come of it?

7. Do you happen to know whether any (other) members of the House are now working actively for or against these measures?
   [*If "yes":*]
   a. Which proposals are involved?
   b. Who is involved?
   c. What are they doing?

8. Have you had any contact with persons or groups outside the House in regard to any of these proposals?
   [If "yes":]
   a. Which proposals were involved?
   b. Who was involved? Are they from your district?
   c. What was said?
   d. Has anything come of it?
9. Is there anything else about this subject that you think we ought to explore in our study?

SOME CONGRESSIONAL ATTITUDES

At various points in the text, we have referred to the members' responses to closed-ended items included as part of the interview. In addition, scales constructed from the responses to items on political party (items 2, 5, 23) and interest groups (items 12, 20, 25) were employed in deriving role typologies discussed in Chapter 5. Because the responses of the eighty-seven general-sample Congressmen to all these items may be of interest to students of legislatures, they are reproduced in full below:

Item	Agree	Tend to Agree	Undecided	Tend to Disagree	Disagree	No Answer
(1) Congress should devote its time to broad policy questions rather than the details of administration.	28%	23%	3%	33%	9%	3%
(2) Under our form of government every individual should take an interest in government directly, not through a political party.	17%	12%	5%	20%	46%	1%
(3) Congressmen should educate the public to help citizens understand issues so they can form opinions and make their opinions known.	78%	13%		3%	4%	1%
(4) The structure of Congress should be designed to protect minority interests from being overrun by hasty majorities.	57%	24%	1%	5%	8%	5%

Item	Agree	Tend to Agree	Undecided	Tend to Disagree	Disagree	No Answer
(5) If a bill is important for his party's record, a member should vote with his party even if it costs him some support in his district.	9%	26%	7%	15%	37%	6%
(6) A Congressman ought to decide how to vote on most issues by asking himself if the proposed law is morally right.	55%	29%	1%	6%	6%	3%
(7) The primary function of House rules and structure must be to allow the majority to work its will.	59%	31%		3%	4%	2%
(8) The two parties should take clear-cut, opposing stands on more of the important and controversial issues.	17%	28%	3%	16%	35%	1%
(9) A Representative ought to work for what his constituents want even though this may not always agree with his personal views.	16%	13%	1%	28%	40%	2%
(10) Congress should play the major role in the making of public policy.	38%	30%	12%	14%	6%	1%
(11) When you come to Washington you have great ideas. But when you are in a committee or on the floor, you are unable to implement your ideas.	17%	30%	1%	28%	22%	2%
(12) On the whole, Congress would work better if there were no interest groups and lobbies trying to influence legislation.	6%	9%	2%	41%	39%	2%
(13) An important part of a Congressman's job should be to go to bat for constituents in their dealings with executive agencies.	31%	45%	2%	13%	8%	1%
(14) Congress and the executive should be equal partners in the making of public policy.	28%	28%	3%	24%	17%	1%

Item	Agree	Tend to Agree	Undecided	Tend to Disagree	Disagree	No Answer
(15) Issues are so technical and time is so short that I often vote without adequate knowledge of the issue.	18%	24%	1%	26%	29%	2%
(16) The job of the Congressman should be to work out compromises among conflicting interests.	26%	44%	1%	15%	13%	2%
(17) I seldom have to sound out my constituents because I think so much like them that I know how to react to almost any proposal.	21%	32%	3%	15%	22%	7%
(18) The executive should play the major role in the making of public policy.	12%	17%	3%	28%	37%	3%
(19) So many groups and individuals want so many different things that it is often difficult to know what stand to take.	8%	22%	1%	26%	39%	3%
(20) Lobbyists and special interests have entirely too much influence in the House.	14%	15%	1%	32%	36%	2%
(21) As a Congressman I can do pretty much what I like here without worrying too much about criticism from my district.	20%	21%		26%	31%	3%
(22) Congress should take an active part in overseeing the administration of public policy.	62%	23%	3%	9%		2%
(23) The best interests of the people would be better served if Congressmen were selected without party labels.	7%	3%	3%	14%	70%	2%
(24) Congress should equip itself with a more extensive professional staff, in order to have its own sources of technical knowledge on the complex problems confronting the nation.	67%	13%	2%	7%	9%	2%

Item	Agree	Tend to Disagree	Undecided	Tend to Agree	Disagree	No Answer
(25) Under our form of government, every individual should seek to influence his Congressman directly, rather than through interest groups and organizations.	25%	35%	3%	16%	18%	2%
(26) The function of Congress should be to ratify or modify legislative proposals initiated by the executive.	1%	12%		20%	66%	2%

NOTES

Preface

[1] Principally in *Congressional Reform: Problems and Prospects,* Michael K. O'Leary, ed. (Hanover, N. H.: Dartmouth Public Affairs Center, 1964); Roger H. Davidson, David M. Kovenock, and Michael K. O'Leary, *Congress in Crisis: Politics and Congressional Reform* (Belmont, Calif.: Wadsworth Publishing Company, 1966); and U.S. Congress, Joint Committee on the Organization of the Congress, *Hearings,* Vol. 5 (89th Congress, 1st session, 1965), pp. 748–782.

[2] *The Legislative System* (New York: John Wiley & Sons, 1962).

Chapter 1

[1] For one attempt to explain recent attention to legislatures see Roger H. Davidson and David M. Kovenock, "The Catfish and the Fisherman: Prescriptive Political Science and Congressional Reform," *American Behavioral Scientist,* 10 (June 1967), 23–27.

[2] The argument summarized here is presented in greater detail in Roger H. Davidson, David M. Kovenock, and Michael K. O'Leary, *Congress in Crisis: Politics and Congressional Reform* (Belmont, Calif.: Wadsworth Publishing Company, 1966), Chaps. 1–2.

[3] Definitions of "politics and the political" are imbedded in much of the contemporary writing on social systems. See Talcott Parsons, *The Social System* (New York: The Free Press of Glencoe, 1951); *Structure and Process in Modern Societies* (New York: The Free Press of Glencoe, 1960); Suzanne Keller, *Beyond the Ruling Class: Strategic Elites in Modern Society* (New York: Random House, 1963); and William C. Mitchell, *Sociological Analysis and Politics* (Englewood Cliffs, N. J.: Prentice-Hall, 1967).

[4] David Easton, *The Political System* (New York: Alfred A. Knopf, 1953), pp. 130 ff.

[5] William C. Mitchell, "The Polity and Society: A Structural-Functional Analysis," *Midwest Journal of Political Science,* 2 (November 1958), 406.

[6] See Leonard A. Lecht, *The Dollar Cost of Our National Goals* (Washington, D. C.: National Planning Association, 1965).

[7] Mitchell, "The Polity and Society," 407.

[8] Davidson, Kovenock, and O'Leary, p. 57.

[9] Mitchell, "The Polity and Society," 413 ff.

[10] *Federalist 48.*

[11] Roland Young, *The American Congress* (New York: Harper & Row, 1958), p. 16.

[12] Robert L. Peabody, "Organization Theory and Legislative Behavior: Bargaining, Hierarchy and Change in the U.S. House of Representatives." Paper presented to the 59th annual meeting of the American Political Science Association (New York: September 4-7, 1963), p. 1. Other exploratory theoretical treatments include Robert A. Dahl, *Politics, Economics, and Welfare* (New York: Harper & Row, 1953), Chaps. 12-13 *et passim;* and Lewis A. Froman, "Organization Theory and the Explanation of Important Characteristics of Congress," *American Political Science Review,* 62 (June 1968), 518-526.

[13] Froman, *op. cit.,* 524.

[14] Quoted in Richard E. Neustadt, *Presidential Power: The Politics of Leadership* (New York: John Wiley & Sons, 1960), p. 22.

[15] *Ibid.,* p. 40.

[16] *Ibid.,* p. 41.

[17] *Ibid.,* p. 53. Italics in original.

[18] Walter Heller, *New Dimensions of Political Economy* (Cambridge, Mass.: Harvard University Press, 1966), p. 47.

[19] Some interesting examples of judicial bargaining are revealed in the usually unpublicized process of drafting opinions. See Alexander M. Bickel, *The Unpublished Opinions of Mr. Justice Brandeis* (Cambridge, Mass.: Belknap Press, 1957). On judicial bargaining in general see Walter F. Murphy, *Elements of Judicial Strategy* (Chicago: University of Chicago Press, 1964).

[20] Froman, *op. cit.,* 518.

[21] T. V. Smith, *The Legislative Way of Life* (Chicago: University of Chicago Press, 1941), p. 4.

[22] William H. Riker, *The Theory of Political Coalitions* (New Haven: Yale University Press, 1962), p. 26.

[23] On this and related subjects see Hanna F. Pitkin, *The Concept of Representation* (Berkeley and Los Angeles: University of California Press, 1967), esp. pp. 118-119, 137 ff.

[24] On the consensual aspects of American society see Louis Hartz, *The Liberal Tradition in America* (New York: Harcourt, Brace & World, 1955). For empirical tests of "rules of the game" under conditions of stress see James W. Prothro and

Charles M. Grigg, "Fundamental Principles of Democracy: Base of Agreement and Disagreement," *Journal of Politics*, 22 (March 1960), 276–294; and Samuel A. Stouffer, *Communism, Conformity and Civil Liberties* (Garden City, N. Y.: Doubleday, 1955), esp. Chap. 2.

[25] Ralph K. Huitt, "The Internal Distribution of Influence: The Senate," in *The Congress and America's Future*, David B. Truman, ed. (Englewood Cliffs, N. J.: Prentice-Hall, 1965), p. 85. For further elaboration of the theme see Huitt's "Democratic Party Leadership in the Senate," *American Political Science Review*, 55 (June 1961), 333–344.

[26] Robin M. Williams, Jr., *American Society: A Sociological Interpretation*, rev. ed. (New York: Alfred A. Knopf, 1960), p. 246.

[27] For further exploration of the concepts of exchange and reciprocity see, for example, John W. Thibaut and Harold H. Kelley, *The Social Psychology of Groups* (New York: John Wiley & Sons, 1959); and Peter M. Blau, *Exchange and Influence in Social Life* (New York: John Wiley & Sons, 1964).

[28] Woodrow Wilson, *Congressional Government* (New York: Meridian Books, 1956), p. 121.

[29] Quoted in Donald R. Matthews, *U.S. Senators and Their World* (Chapel Hill: University of North Carolina Press, 1960), p. 100.

[30] Sar A. Levitan, *Federal Aid to Depressed Areas* (Baltimore: Johns Hopkins University Press, 1964), pp. 26–27.

[31] David B. Truman, *The Governmental Process* (New York: Alfred A. Knopf, 1951), p. 368.

[32] Matthews, *op. cit.*, pp. 99–101.

[33] *Ibid.*, Chap. 5. On the House of Representatives see Charles L. Clapp, *The Congressman: His Work As He Sees It* (Washington, D. C.: The Brookings Institution, 1963), esp. Chaps. 1–3.

[34] Thibaut and Kelley, *op. cit.*, pp. 142–147; Ralph Linton, *The Study of Man* (New York: Appleton-Century-Crofts, 1936), pp. 114 ff.; Robert K. Merton, *Social Structure and Social Theory* (New York: The Free Press of Glencoe, 1957), pp. 369–371.

CHAPTER 2

[1] Alexander Hamilton or James Madison, *Federalist 57*.

[2] *Ibid.*

[3] Roland Young, *The American Congress* (New York: Harper & Row, 1958), p. 285.

[4] Suzanne Keller, *Beyond the Ruling Class: Strategic Elites in Modern Society* (New York: Random House, 1963), p. 90.

[5] For a discussion of the relevance of such a study see Donald R. Matthews, *The Social Background of Political Decision-Makers* (Garden City, N. Y.: Doubleday, 1954), esp. Chap. 1. By analyzing the variables of social status and prior political

experience, Matthews has attempted to devise a typology of Senatorial behavior patterns. See his *U.S. Senators and Their World* (Chapel Hill: University of North Carolina Press, 1960), pp. 58–67, 103–109, 157–158.

[6] David B. Truman, *The Governmental Process* (New York: Alfred A. Knopf, 1951), p. 332.

[7] Stephen K. Bailey, *Congress Makes a Law* (New York: Columbia University Press, 1950), p. 190.

[8] George B. Galloway, *History of the House of Representatives* (New York: Thomas Y. Crowell, 1961), p. 35.

[9] Matthews, *U.S. Senators and Their World*, p. 33.

[10] See, for example, Charles S. Hyneman, "Who Makes Our Laws?" *Political Science Quarterly*, 55 (1940), 556–581; Joseph A. Schlesinger, "Lawyers and American Politics: A Clarified View," *Midwest Journal of Political Science*, 1 (May 1957), 26–39; David Gold, "Lawyers in Politics," *Pacific Sociological Review*, 4 (Fall 1961), 84–86; and Matthews, *The Social Background of Political Decision-Makers*, pp. 30–32.

[11] Matthews, *Social Background*, p. 30.

[12] Schlesinger, *op. cit.*

[13] Hyneman, *op. cit.*; Gold, *op. cit.*; Matthews, *Social Background*, p. 30.

[14] Harold D. Lasswell and M. S. McDougal, "Legal Education and Public Policy," in *The Analysis of Political Behaviour*, Lasswell, ed. (London: Kegan Paul, Trench, Trubner & Co., 1947), p. 27.

[15] The phrase is from Heinz Eulau and John Sprague, *Lawyers in Politics: A Study in Professional Convergence* (Indianapolis: Bobbs-Merrill, 1964).

[16] On the subject of doctors in politics see William A. Glaser, "Doctors in Politics," *American Journal of Sociology*, 66 (November 1960), 230–245.

[17] See Joseph A. Schlesinger, *Ambition and Politics* (Chicago: Rand-McNally, 1966), pp. 177–179.

[18] See Galloway, *op. cit.*, pp. 35–36.

[19] James S. Young, *The Washington Community, 1800–1828* (New York: Columbia University Press, 1966), p. 92.

[20] Galloway, *op. cit.*, p. 35.

[21] Matthews, *U.S. Senators*, pp. 40–42.

[22] *Ibid.*, p. 66.

[23] Charles O. Paullin, "The First Elections Under the Constitution," *Iowa Journal of History and Politics*, 3 (January 1904), 28.

[24] Galloway, *op. cit.*, p. 33.

[25] Matthews, *U.S. Senators*, pp. 55 ff.; Schlesinger, *Ambition and Politics*, pp. 92 ff.

[26] See Young, *The Washington Community.*

[27] See Schlesinger, *Ambition and Politics.*

[28] Hamilton or Madison, *Federalist 56.*

[29] See Paullin, *op. cit.,* p. 13.

[30] See Andrew Hacker, "The Elected and the Anointed," *American Political Science Review,* 55 (September 1961), 544–545; and Samuel P. Huntington, "Congressional Responses to the Twentieth Century," in *The Congress and America's Future,* David B. Truman, ed. (Englewood Cliffs, N. J.: Prentice-Hall, 1965), pp. 12–16.

[31] Matthews, *U.S. Senators,* pp. 35, 40–42.

[32] See Chap. 4 below, as well as Roger H. Davidson, "Congress and the Presidency: The Race for Representation," in *Congress, The First Branch,* Alfred de Grazia, ed. (Garden City, N. Y.: Doubleday Anchor Books, 1967).

[33] See, among others, Matthews, *U.S. Senators,* esp. Chap. 5; Richard F. Fenno, Jr., "The Internal Distribution of Influence: The House," in *The Congress and America's Future;* and William S. White's volumes *Citadel* (New York: Harper & Row, 1956) and *Home Place* (Boston: Houghton Mifflin, 1965).

[34] See Nelson W. Polsby, "The Institutionalization of the House of Representatives," *American Political Science Review,* 62 (March 1968), 146–147.

[35] Young, *The Washington Community,* p. 89.

[36] Polsby, *loc. cit.*

[37] Polsby, *op. cit.*

[38] Hamilton or Madison, *Federalist 53.*

[39] *Ibid.*

[40] T. Richard Witmer, "The Aging of the House," *Political Science Quarterly,* 79 (December 1964), 526–541.

[41] *Ibid.,* 529.

[42] U.S. Bureau of the Census, *Historical Statistics of the United States, Colonial Times to 1957* (Washington, D. C.: U.S. Government Printing Office, 1960), p. 24; also *Continuation to 1962 and Revisions* (1965), p. 5.

[43] Young, *The Washington Community,* p. 57.

[44] *Ibid.,* p. 89.

[45] Randall B. Ripley, *Party Leaders in the House of Representatives* (Washington, D. C.: The Brookings Institution, 1967), pp. 51–52.

[46] Polsby, *op. cit.,* pp. 147 ff.

[47] Huntington, *op. cit.,* p. 11.

[48] See Schlesinger, *Ambition and Politics,* pp. 92–93.

[49] See Milton C. Cummings, Jr., *Congressmen and the Electorate* (New York: The Free Press of Glencoe, 1966), esp. pp. 68–72.

[50] See H. Douglas Price, "The Electoral Arena," in *The Congress and America's Future*, pp. 42–45; and *Congressional Quarterly Weekly Report* (December 7, 1962), pp. 2225–2230.

[51] Charles O. Jones, "Inter-Party Competition for Congressional Seats," *Western Political Quarterly*, 17 (September 1964), 461–476. See also Cummings, *op. cit.*, pp. 186–187; and Lewis A. Froman, *Congressmen and Their Constituencies* (Chicago: Rand-McNally, 1963), pp. 81–82.

[52] Schlesinger, *Ambition and Politics*, pp. 62–65.

[53] On the relation of public assessment of Congress and electoral turnover see Roger H. Davidson, David M. Kovenock, and Michael K. O'Leary, *Congress in Crisis: Politics and Congressional Reform* (Belmont, Calif.: Wadsworth Publishing Company, 1966), pp. 54–55.

[54] Stuart A. Rice, *Quantitative Methods in Politics* (New York: Alfred A. Knopf, 1928), p. 306.

[55] See the comments of incumbents as cited in Charles L. Clapp, *The Congressman: His Work As He Sees It* (Washington, D. C.: The Brookings Institution, 1963), pp. 485 ff.

CHAPTER 3

[1] In *Toward a General Theory of Action*, Talcott Parsons and Edward A. Shils, eds. (Cambridge, Mass.: Harvard University Press, 1951), p. 190. Italics in original.

[2] John W. Thibaut and Harold H. Kelley, *The Social Psychology of Groups* (New York: John Wiley & Sons, 1959), p. 148. The various meanings of the concept and the resulting problems are surveyed in Lionel J. Nieman and James W. Hughes, "The Problem of the Concept of Role—A Re-survey of the Literature," *Social Forces*, 30 (December 1951), 141–149. A comprehensive review of the history and usage of the concept is found in *Role Theory: Concepts and Research*, Bruce J. Biddle and Edwin J. Thomas, eds. (New York: John Wiley & Sons, 1966), pp. 3–63.

[3] Ralph Linton, *The Study of Man* (New York: Appleton-Century-Crofts, 1936), p. 114. For a modification of Linton's definitions in light of more recent thought see, for example, Robert K. Merton, *Social Theory and Social Structure* (New York: The Free Press of Glencoe, 1957), pp. 369 ff.

[4] In *Bureaucracy and Political Development*, Joseph La Polambara, ed. (Princeton: Princeton University Press, 1963), p. 168.

[5] For the concept of role-set see Merton, *loc. cit.*

[6] Adapted from John Wahlke *et al.*, *The Legislative System* (New York: John Wiley & Sons, 1962), p. 14. An alternative conceptualization is found in Malcolm Jewell and Samuel Patterson, *The Legislative Process in the United States* (New York: Random House, 1966), p. 384.

[7] Wahlke *et al.*, *op. cit.*, p. 11.

[8] *Ibid.*, p. 12.

[9] *Ibid.*, p. 11. Matthews' Senate folkways are consensual roles of this type. See Donald R. Matthews, *U.S. Senators and Their World* (Chapel Hill: University of North Carolina Press, 1960), Chap. 5.

[10] See Thibaut and Kelley, *op. cit.*, pp. 144-145; and *Role Theory: Concepts and Research*, pp. 30 ff.

[11] Neal Gross, Ward S. Mason, and Alexander McEachern, *Explorations in Role Analysis* (New York: John Wiley & Sons, 1958), Chap. 3.

[12] However, see Roger H. Davidson, David M. Kovenock, and Michael K. O'Leary, *Congress in Crisis: Politics and Congressional Reform* (Belmont, Calif.: Wadsworth Publishing Company, 1966), Chap. 2; Carl D. McMurray and Malcolm B. Parsons, "Public Attitudes Toward the Representational Role of Legislators and Judges," *Midwest Journal of Political Science*, 9 (May 1965), 167-185; and M. Kent Jennings, Milton C. Cummings, and Franklin P. Kilpatrick, "Trusted Leaders: Perceptions of Appointed Federal Officials," *Public Opinion Quarterly*, 30 (Fall 1966), 380-381.

[13] Wahlke *et al.*, p. 8.

[14] *Ibid.*, pp. 32-33, 239-240. See also Gross, Mason, and McEachern, *op. cit.*, *passim*.

[15] Their survey instrument is reproduced in Wahlke *et al.*, *op cit.*, pp. 492-504.

[16] *Ibid.*, App. 1.

[17] *Ibid.*, pp. 12, 242.

[18] *Ibid.*, p. 260.

[19] *Ibid.*, p. 259.

[20] See Jennings, Cummings, and Kilpatrick, *op. cit.*, p. 381.

[21] This definition of the Ritualist is somewhat broader than that given by Wahlke and his associates, *op cit.*, p. 252.

[22] Quoted in Charles L. Clapp, *The Congressman: His Work As He Sees It* (Washington, D. C.: The Brookings Institution, 1963), p. 23.

[23] Frank E. Smith, *Congressman from Mississippi* (New York: Pantheon Books, 1964), pp. 129-130.

[24] Wahlke *et al.*, *op. cit.*, p. 249.

[25] James David Barber, *The Lawmakers: Recruitment and Adaptation to Legislative Life* (New Haven: Yale University Press, 1965).

[26] Smith, *op. cit.*, p. 127. See also Clapp, *op. cit.*, pp. 86-87.

[27] See, however, John B. McConaughy, "Certain Personality Factors of State Legislators in South Carolina," *American Political Science Review*, 44 (December 1950), 897–903; and Barber, *op. cit.*

[28] See Heinz Eulau and John D. Sprague, *Lawyers in Politics: A Study in Professional Convergence* (Indianapolis: Bobbs-Merrill, 1964), Chap. 4.

[29] *Ibid.*, p. 97.

[30] For a definition of the "conservative coalition" as well as data concerning support of that coalition, see *Congressional Quarterly Almanac, 1964* (Washington, D. C.: Congressional Quarterly Service, 1965), pp. 745–753.

[31] Davidson, Kovenock, and O'Leary, *op. cit.*, pp. 85–86.

[32] The classification used here, which divides districts into urban, suburban, rural, and mixed, was developed by *Congressional Quarterly* and described in *Congressional Quarterly Weekly Report*, Part I (August 21, 1964), pp. 1784–1798.

[33] See Davidson, Kovenock, and O'Leary, *op. cit.*, p. 77. A thoughtful discussion of the problem is found in Raymond A. Bauer, Ithiel de Sola Pool, and Lewis A. Dexter, *American Business and Public Policy* (New York: Atherton Press, 1963), pp. 405–413.

[34] John S. Saloma examined the work schedules of 160 Congressional offices during the 89th Congress. Preliminary reports of his study are found in Donald G. Tacheron and Morris K. Udall, *The Job of the Congressman* (Indianapolis: Bobbs-Merrill, 1966), pp. 280–288; and John S. Saloma, "The Job of a Congressman: Some Perspectives on Time and Information" (1967, forthcoming). Saloma's sample of members, however, is open to considerable question, especially in its over-representation of Republicans and freshmen.

[35] Saloma, pp. 7–8.

[36] Tacheron and Udall, *op. cit.*, p. 285.

[37] *Ibid.*

[38] See, for example, Carl F. Hawver, *The Congressman's Conception of His Role* (Washington, D. C.: privately published, 1963).

[39] David S. Broder, "Portrait of a Typical Congressman," *The New York Times Magazine* (October 7, 1962).

[40] Jim Wright, *You and Your Congressman* (New York: Coward-McCann, 1965), p. 14. See also Clapp, *op. cit.*, pp. 51–55.

[41] Saloma, p. 24.

[42] On the relative desirability and differing work norms of the Appropriations, Rules, and Ways and Means Committees see, respectively: Richard F. Fenno, Jr., "The Appropriations Committee As a Political System," *American Political Science Review*, 56 (June 1962), 310–324; Robert L. Peabody, "The Enlarged Rules Committee," in *New Perspectives on the House of Representatives*, Robert L. Peabody and Nelson W. Polsby, eds. (Chicago: Rand-McNally, 1963), pp. 129–164; and John F.

Manley, "The House Ways and Means Committee: Conflict Management in a Congressional Committee," *American Political Science Review*, 59 (December 1965), 927–939. And see generally Nicholas A. Masters, "Committee Assignments in the House of Representatives," *American Political Science Review*, 55 (June 1961), 345–357.

[43] Saloma, p. 23.

CHAPTER 4

[1] One exposition of theories of Presidential representation is found in Edward S. Corwin, *The President: Office and Powers*, 4th ed. (New York: New York University. Press, 1957), Chap. 1.

[2] Norton E. Long, "Bureaucracy and Constitutionalism," *American Political Science Review*, 46 (September 1952), 808–818.

[3] See, for example, Locke's *Second Treatise on Civil Government*, Sir Ernest Barker, ed. (London: Oxford University Press, 1947), pp. 111–112, 120–121, *et passim.*

[4] Samuel Huntington, "Congressional Responses to the Twentieth Century," in *The Congress and America's Future*, David B. Truman, ed. (Englewood Cliffs, N. J.: Prentice-Hall, 1965), p. 16.

[5] Alfred de Grazia, *Public and Republic* (New York: Alfred A. Knopf, 1951), p. 4.

[6] See, for example, Donald R. Matthews, *The Social Background of Political Decision-Makers* (Garden City, N. Y.: Doubleday, 1955).

[7] Two studies that employ party and constituency variables are: Julius Turner, *Party and Constituency: Pressures on Congress* (Baltimore: Johns Hopkins University Press, 1952); and David H. Mayhew, *Party Loyalty Among Congressmen* (Cambridge, Mass.: Harvard University Press, 1966).

[8] James Wilson, *Works*, James D. Andrews, ed. (Chicago: Callaghan & Co., 1896), Vol. I, p. 389. Hanna F. Pitkin's distinction between representation as "standing for" and representation as "activity" parallels the distinction made here. See *The Concept of Representation* (Berkeley and Los Angeles: University of California Press, 1967), esp. pp. 112 ff.

[9] Seymour M. Lipset, "Party Systems and the Representation of Social Groups," *European Journal of Sociology*, 1 (1960), 51.

[10] See David M. Kovenock, "A Communications Audit of Members of the U.S. House of Representatives." Paper presented to the 60th annual meeting of the American Political Science Association (Chicago: September 8–12, 1964).

[11] Raymond A. Bauer, Ithiel de Sola Pool, and Lewis A. Dexter, *American Business and Public Policy* (New York: Atherton Press, 1963).

[12] Angus Campbell *et al., Elections and the Political Order* (New York: The Free Press of Glencoe, 1966), Chap. 16. Originally published as "Constituency Influence in Congress," *American Political Science Review*, 57 (March 1963), 45–56. See also a methodological comment on this study, Charles F. Cnudde and Donald J. McCrone,

"The Linkage Between Constituency Attitudes and Congressional Voting Behavior: A Causal Model," *American Political Science Review*, 60 (March 1966), 66–72.

[13] In the terminology of Wahlke and his associates, "representational roles" and "areal roles." Again we must acknowledge indebtedness to these investigators for their concepts and terms developed in *The Legislative System* (New York: John Wiley & Sons, 1962).

[14] The "law of anticipated reactions" has been developed and explained by Carl J. Friedrich in many of his writings. His most recent exposition of the subject is in his *Man and His Government* (New York: McGraw-Hill, 1963), esp. pp. 203–205.

[15] See David M. Kovenock, "Communications and Influence in the House of Representatives: Some Preliminary Statistical Snapshots." Paper presented to the 63rd annual meeting of the American Political Science Association (Chicago: September 6–9, 1967).

[16] Speech to the Electors of Bristol (November 3, 1774), in *Burke's Politics*, Ross J. S. Hoffman and Paul Levack, eds. (New York: Alfred A. Knopf, 1959), pp. 114–116.

[17] John F. Kennedy, *Profiles in Courage* (New York: Harper & Row, 1954), pp. 21–37.

[18] See also Richard Rose, *Politics in England* (Boston: Little, Brown, 1964), pp. 166–167, and the works cited there.

[19] Daniel J. Boorstin, *The Americans: The Colonial Experience* (New York: Random House, 1958), pp. 118–119.

[20] See, for example, James Mill, *An Essay on Government*, Currin V. Shields, ed. (New York: Library of Liberal Arts, 1955), esp. pp. 67 ff. The controversy is reviewed in *The Representative: Trustee? Delegate? Partisan? Politico?*, Neal Riemer, ed. (Boston: D. C. Heath, 1967), pp. 109–116 *et passim*.

[21] The evidence, though far from conclusive, points to this conclusion. See Carl D. McMurray and Malcolm B. Parsons, "Public Attitudes Toward the Representational Role of Legislators and Judges," *Midwest Journal of Political Science*, 9 (May 1965), 167–185.

[22] *Congressional Record* (90th Congress, 1st session), A2930 (June 12, 1967, daily edition).

[23] Roger H. Davidson, David M. Kovenock, and Michael K. O'Leary, *Congress in Crisis: Politics and Congressional Reform*. (Belmont, Calif.: Wadsworth Publishing Company, 1966), pp. 57–59.

[24] See Miller and Stokes, in Campbell, *et al., op. cit.*

[25] Heinz Eulau and LeRoy C. Ferguson, "The Role of the Representative: Some Empirical Observations on the Theory of Edmund Burke," *American Political Science Review*, 53 (September 1959), 742–756.

[26] Quoted in Charles Mangel, "Paul Douglas: Man Ahead of His Time," *Look* (June 13, 1967), 106.

[27] Lewis A. Dexter, "The Representative and His District," in *New Perspectives on the House of Representatives*, Robert L. Peabody and Nelson W. Polsby, eds. (Chicago: Rand McNally, 1963), pp. 4–5. See also Bauer *et al., op. cit.,* Chaps. 29–30; L. E. Gleeck, "96 Congressmen Make Up Their Minds," *Public Opinion Quarterly*, 4 (March 1940), 3–24; and George W. Hartmann, "Judgments of State Legislators Concerning Public Opinion," *Journal of Social Psychology*, 21 (February 1945), 105–114.

[28] Wahlke *et al., op. cit.,* p. 281. For figures on the Pennsylvania legislature see Frank J. Sorauf, *Party and Representation* (New York: Atherton Press, 1963), p. 124. Samuel C. Patterson's unpublished study of the Wisconsin legislature is referred to in Malcolm E. Jewell and Samuel C. Patterson, *The Legislative Process in the United States* (New York: Random House, 1966), pp. 398–399. Donald P. Sprengel's unpublished study of the North Carolina legislature is cited in *American Legislative Behavior*, Samuel C. Patterson, ed. (Princeton: D. Van Nostrand, 1968), pp. 214–216.

[29] Wahlke *et al., op. cit.,* p. 286.

[30] Sorauf, *op. cit.,* p. 126. See also Wilder Crane, Jr., "The Legislative Struggle in Wisconsin: Decision Making in the 1957 Wisconsin Assembly." Unpublished doctoral dissertation, University of Wisconsin–Madison, 1959.

[31] On this point see Pitkin, *op. cit.,* p. 165.

[32] See Miller and Stokes, *op. cit.,* and the same authors' "Party Government and the Saliency of Congress," in Campbell *et al., op. cit.,* pp. 198 ff.

[33] See Dexter, *loc. cit.*

[34] See Rose, *loc. cit.*

[35] For a thorough exposition of these relationships see Milton C. Cummings, Jr., *Congressmen and the Electorate* (New York: The Free Press, 1966).

[36] See the discussion in Chap. 2.

[37] James N. Rosenau, *National Leadership and Foreign Policy* (Princeton: Princeton University Press, 1963), pp. 30–31. Expressions on this point are so common that any listing is bound to be partial. See Huntington, *loc. cit.;* James McGregor Burns, *Congress on Trial* (New York: Harper & Row, 1949), esp. Chap. 1; Robert A. Dahl, *Congress and Foreign Policy* (New York: Harcourt, Brace & World, 1950), esp. Chaps. 1–2; Andrew Hacker, "The Elected and the Anointed," *American Political Science Review*, 55 (September 1961), 539–549; and Daniel M. Berman, *In Congress Assembled* (New York: Macmillan, 1964), esp. pp. 66–69, 402–403.

[38] William S. White, *Home Place* (Boston: Houghton Mifflin, 1965), pp. 54 ff.

[39] See Eulau and Ferguson, *op. cit.,* p. 753.

[40] The statistics are from *Congressional Quarterly Almanac, 1962* (Washington, D. C.: Congressional Quarterly Service, 1963), pp. 1163–1168.

[41] The classification of districts by degree of urbanization is drawn from *Congressional Quarterly Weekly Report*, Part I (August 21, 1964), pp. 1784–1798.

[42] See, for example, Mayhew, *op. cit.*

[43] On this subject generally see Cummings, *op. cit.*

[44] See Lewis A. Froman, *Congressmen and Their Constituencies* (Chicago: Rand-McNally, 1963), Chap. 2.

[45] Charles A. Vanik (D-Ohio), in *Congressional Record* (90th Congress, 1st session), H7608 (June 21, 1967, daily edition).

[46] Kovenock, "Communications and Influence in the House of Representatives."

CHAPTER 5

[1] A useful set of role typologies drawn from the literature is found in Malcolm E. Jewell and Samuel C. Patterson, *The Legislative Process in the United States* (New York: Random House, 1966), pp. 385–387.

[2] David B. Truman, *The Congressional Party* (New York: John Wiley & Sons, 1959), esp. Chap. 8. See also Mark Kesselman, "Presidential Leadership in Congress on Foreign Policy," *Midwest Journal of Political Science*, 9 (November 1965), 401–406.

[3] V. O. Key, Jr., *Politics, Parties and Pressure Groups*, 5th ed. (New York: Thomas Y. Crowell, 1964), p. 682.

[4] Committee on Political Parties, American Political Science Association, "Toward a More Responsible Two-Party System," *American Political Science Review*, 44 (September 1950), Supp. More recently, reform-minded members of both houses have urged a greater measure of party organization and cohesion. See Richard Bolling, *House Out of Order* (New York: E. P. Dutton, 1964).

[5] See Julius Turner, *Party and Constituency: Pressures on Congress* (Baltimore: Johns Hopkins University Press, 1951); and Duncan MacRae, Jr., *Dimensions of Congressional Voting* (Berkeley and Los Angeles: University of California Press, 1958).

[6] Lewis A. Froman, Jr., *Congressmen and Their Constituencies* (Chicago: Rand McNally, 1963), Chap. 7.

[7] See also Warren Miller and Donald E. Stokes, "Constituency Influence in Congress," in Angus Campbell et al., *Elections and the Political Order*, (New York: John Wiley & Sons, 1967), Chap. 16.

[8] These propositions are summarized in Randall B. Ripley, *Party Leaders in the House of Representatives* (Washington, D. C.: The Brookings Institution, 1967), p. 9. Ripley adds, however, that "there is almost no material on the members' perceptions of the leaders, their activities, and the meaning of party loyalty." See also David R. Mayhew, *Party Loyalty Among Congressmen* (Cambridge, Mass.: Harvard University Press, 1965), Chap. 6.

[9] Ripley, pp. 141–142.

[10] See *Congressional Quarterly Almanac*, 20 (Washington, D. C.: Congressional Quarterly Service, 1964), pp. 740–741.

[11] See Truman, *op. cit.*, pp. 308 ff.

[12] See Kesselman, *loc. cit.*

[13] Ripley, p. 156.

[14] Irwin N. Gertzog, "Frustration and Adaptation: The Adjustment of Minority Freshmen to the Congressional Experience." Paper delivered at the annual meeting of the American Political Science Association (September 6–10, 1966), pp. 18 ff. The discussion here closely follows Gertzog's findings.

[15] On committee assignment procedures see Nicholas A. Masters, "Committee Assignments in the House of Representatives," *American Political Science Review*, 55 (June 1961), 345–357.

[16] Gertzog, pp. 18–21.

[17] *Ibid.*, p. 18.

[18] Ripley, pp. 156–157.

[19] See Froman, *op. cit.*, p. 114; and Raymond Wolfinger and Joan Heifitz, "Safe Seats, Seniority, and Power in Congress," *American Political Science Review*, 64 (June 1965), p. 341.

[20] Classification of district type is based on the categories used in *Congressional Quarterly Almanac, 1962* (Washington, D. C.: Congressional Quarterly Service, 1963), pp. 1170–1184.

[21] Ripley's examination of party voting yielded somewhat different results. See Ripley, pp. 155–156.

[22] See John Wahlke *et al.*, *The Legislative System* (New York: John Wiley & Sons, 1962), Chap. 8.

[23] See Mayhew, *op. cit.*

[24] For a statement that comes very close to this position see Earl Lathem, *The Group Basis of Politics* (Ithaca, N. Y.: Cornell University Press, 1952), p. 35.

[25] The most comprehensive and, on the whole, the most balanced view of the role of interest groups remains David B. Truman's *The Governmental Process* (New York: Alfred A. Knopf, 1951). Truman's comments on the limitations of the "group" approach are found in a letter in *American Political Science Review*, 54 (June 1960), 494–495. Other important items in the literature include Raymond A. Bauer, Ithiel de Sola Pool, and Lewis A. Dexter, *American Business and Public Policy* (New York: Atherton Press, 1963), esp. Part 4; and Lester Milbrath, *The Washington Lobbyists* (Chicago: Rand McNally, 1963).

[26] In addition to the works cited above, this paragraph draws upon E. E. Schattschneider, *The Semi-sovereign People* (New York: Holt, Rinehart & Winston, 1960); and Andrew M. Scott and Margaret A. Hunt, *Congress and Lobbies* (Chapel Hill: University of North Carolina Press, 1965).

[27] These items were adapted from Wahlke *et al.*, pp. 502–503.

[28] Wahlke *et al.*, p. 331.

[29] Scott and Hunt, *op. cit.*, p. 69.

[30] See David R. Derge, "The Lawyer as Decision Maker," *Journal of Politics*, 21 (August, 1959), 408–433.

[31] See Wahlke *et al.*, p. 329 *n.*

[32] Similar findings and reasoning are presented in. Scott and Hunt, *op. cit.*, pp. 65–69.

[33] Wahlke *et al.*, p. 341.

[34] See Froman, *loc. cit.* In the population at large, group affiliation and political participation are more common among groupings with "Republican" characteristics than those with "Democratic" characteristics. See Angus Campbell *et al., The American Voter* (New York: John Wiley & Sons, 1960), Chap. 12.

CHAPTER 6

[1] David B. Truman, *The Congressional Party* (New York: John Wiley & Sons, 1959), pp. 95 ff., 115 ff., *et passim.*

[2] See Donald R. Matthews, *U.S. Senators and Their World* (Chapel Hill: University of North Carolina Press, 1960), Chap. 5; and Ralph K. Huitt, "The Outsider in the Senate: An Alternative Role," *American Political Science Review*, 55 (September 1961), 566–575.

[3] Richard F. Fenno, Jr., "The Internal Distribution of Influence: The House," in *The Congress and America's Future*, David B. Truman, ed. (Englewood Cliffs, N. J.: Prentice-Hall, 1965), pp. 71 ff.

[4] Quoted in Booth Mooney, *Mr. Speaker* (Chicago: Follett Publishing Company, 1964), p. 166.

[5] Matthews, *op. cit.;* and William S. White, *Citadel* (New York: Harper & Row, 1956).

[6] Quoted in Mooney, *op. cit.*, p. 184.

[7] See Roger H. Davidson, David M. Kovenock, and Michael K. O'Leary, *Congress in Crisis: Politics and Congressional Reform* (Belmont, Calif.: Wadsworth Publishing Company, 1966), Chap. 2.

[8] M. Kent Jennings, Milton C. Cummings, Jr., and Franklin P. Kilpatrick, "Trusted Leaders: Perceptions of Appointed Federal Officials," *Public Opinion Quarterly*, 30 (Fall 1966), 380–381.

[9] Carl D. McMurray and Malcolm B. Parsons, "Public Attitudes Toward the Representational Roles of Legislators and Judges," *Midwest Journal of Political Science*, 9 (May 1965), 167–185.

[10] Again, see Warren E. Miller and Donald E. Stokes, "Constituency Influence in Congress," *American Political Science Review*, 57 (March 1963), 45–56.

[11] Phrase quoted by James S. Young in *The Washington Community, 1800–1828* (New York: Columbia University Press, 1966), p. 33. The phrase is from Alexander Hamilton, *Federalist 27.*

Appendix

[1]*Congress in Crisis: Politics and Congressional Reform* (Belmont, Calif.: Wadsworth Publishing Company, 1966), Appendix A.

[2] John C. Wahlke *et al.*, *The Legislative System* (New York: John Wiley & Sons, 1962); James A. Robinson, *Congress and Foreign Policy-Making* (Homewood, Ill.: Dorsey Press, 1962); Warren E. Miller and Donald E. Stokes, "Constituency Influence in Congress," *American Political Science Review*, 57 (March 1963), 45–56.

[3] Wahlke *et al.*, *op. cit.*, Chaps. 1 and 11; Appendices 1 and 6.

[4] Davidson, Kovenock and O'Leary, *op. cit.*, Appendix B.

INDEX